Mad Ads:
Be Everywhere
Madison Avenue Advertising on a Main Street Budget

By David T. Fagan and Aaron Halderman

1. 107 ways to advertise your business quickly and inexpensively – including a comprehensive list of resources

2. Track your results as profitability and watch your business grow!

3. Moments that Changed Advertising: big campaigns from big corporations that forever changed how we market and advertise today

Mad Ads: Be Everywhere
Madison Avenue Advertising on a Main Street Budget
Copyright © 2010 by David T. Fagan

Published by On the Inside Press
ISBN: 978-0-9829153-4-9

Dedication

To Our Team:

Carli Smith
Billy Fischbach
Kurt Perenchio
Jamie Wingate

- DTF & AH

Acknowledgements

Thanks Manhattan and Las Vegas...

This book simply couldn't have happened without so many people. First and foremost is the amazing family that surrounds us: Our amazing wives, Jill and Brea, whose unconditional support allows us to accomplish so much; our parents, without them we wouldn't be who we are today; our siblings, who were our best friends growing up. And our amazing children, who show us daily how to love.

After family, there is an incredible group of talented people who have helped and been an influence over the years. We'd like to acknowledge the following for their contributions to our lives and this book:

Adam Daniels	Dan Bradbury	Harry Dent
Adam Ross	Dan Christianson	Jairek Robbins
Adam Urbanski	Dan Kennedy	James Bridges
AJ Puedan	Darcy Juarez	James Thompson
Alexis Neely	Darrin Mish	Jarrod Morris
Alfred Lin	Dave Lee	Jay Conrad Levinson
Alyssa Peterson	Dave Van Hoose	Jean-Guy Franceour
Amy Levinson	David Atkinson	Jeannie Levinson
Andrew Locke	David Frey	Jeff Mask
Andy Harrington	De Anna Rogers	Joel Bauer
Ben Glass	Debbie Woodruff	Joey Bridges
Ben Morris	Dustin Lunt	John Assaraf
Bill Glazer	Dustin Mathews	John DeSantiago
BJ Savage	Ed Diamond	John Jantsch
Bob Diamond	Ed O' Keefe	John Maxwell
Bob Proctor	Ed Rush	Jonathan Jay
Brad Fallon	Eric Larson	Jonathan Mizel
Brad Martineau	Eric Martineau	Jordan Adler
Brandon Barnum	Garret Miles	Jordan Hall
Brian Johnson	Gerald Romine	Jordan Mauzy
Brian Tracy	Gerry Roberts	Josh Bailey
Brock Felt	Glen Ormiston	Konrad Sopielnikow
Christal Galaviz	Greg Stanley	Kyle Leavitt
Clate Mask	Gregg Cochran	Larry Benet
Colin Daymude	Dr. Hailey Purles	Liora Mendeloff
Cory Hodnett	Harry Cornelius	Lori Elgin

Lori Hart
Lynn Rose
Marc Chesley
Mark Evans
Martin Howie
Matt Wingate
Michael Levine
Michael Weiss
Mike Warren
Miranda Larsen
Nate Leavitt
Neal Lambert
Nick James
Nick Nanton
Nicole Shoots
Paul Lonsford
Paul Schween
Perry Marshall
Reed Allmand
Richard Seppala
Rick Grunden
Rob Dickson
Roger Salam
Ron LeGrand
Ross Hamilton
Ryan Chapman
Ryan Deiss
Ryan Garey

Ryan Peterson
Sam Blackham
Scott Martineau
Scott Rholeder
Scott Schumann
Scotty Saks
Sean Chapman
Sean Greeley
Sharon Jakubecy
Sheila Farragher-Gemma
Simon Hedley
Sohail Khan
Steve Hoffstetter
Steve Sipress
Stevi Sullivan
Ted Thomas
Than Merrill
Tiffany Poole
Tom Foster
Tony Hsieh
Travis Merrick
Travis Tollestrup
Trent Chapman
Tyler Garns
Wes Wolcott
Woody Oakes
Yanik Silver

...MAD ADVERTISERS EACH AND EVERY ONE

Finally, the book you are about to read would not have happened without
the fantastic Candace Moorehouse, who was instrumental in helping us
write this book. This would not be the book it is without the thoughtful
comments of those who gave us feedback.

To all of these wonderful people, we are deeply grateful.

Contents

Dedication i

Acknowledgements ii

Forward 11

Introduction: Mad Ads and the Mad Men Who Started It All 13

Chapter One: Every Journey Starts with a Road Map 25

    Goals & Objectives 26

    Target Market 29

    Methodology 33

    Budget 39

Chapter Two: Creative Advertising – The Seduction of the Customer 42

    Focus on the Familiar 43

    Make Them Pay Attention; Make Them Act 45

    Pump Up Your Creative Muscle 47

    Mix It Up 50

Chapter Three: The Importance of Tracking and Testing, then Testing Some More 53

    The Time Commitment 54

    The Repetition and Consistency Commitment 55

    Tracking 56

    Testing 61

Chapter Four: Internet Marketing – Turn On, Plug In, Make Profits 66

    Websites 69

    Social Media 77

Pay Per Click Advertising Campaigns 85

More Online Advertising Opportunities 89

Chapter Five: Signage – Getting People to Take a Second Look   94

Indoor Signage 97

Outdoor Signage 100

Chapter Six: What's in a Name? Branding and Promotion 109

Visuals 115

Tangible Items 118

Broadcasting 124

Teaching & Training 127

Chapter Seven: Print – Not Just Black & White 131

The Basics 136

Print Advertisements..139

More Forms of Printed Advertising 144

Chapter Eight: Direct Marketing – Hitting the Bull's Eye When Targeting Prospects 149

Direct Mail Marketing...152

Other Forms of Direct Marketing 159

Chapter Nine: People Connections – Who's Talking About You?   164

Chapter Ten: Five More Creative Ways to Advertise Your Small Business 174

Chapter Eleven: Mad Ads for Any Size Budget and the Necessary Resources 179

The 107 Mad Ads Methods for Main Street Budgets.................181

Resources 184

Online Advertising 184

Signage..192

Aerial Advertising 193

Branding and Promotion 194

Print 195

Direct Marketing... 198

People Connections.. 199

Creative Extras.. 200

Chapter Twelve: An Advertising Crystal Ball – Media, Message, and
   Methodology of the Future 202

David T. Fagan & Aaron Halderman

Forward

As America's Small Business Owner, I represent over 99% of all employers in the United States. I pay out $1.5 trillion to employees, almost one third of the national payroll.

I <u>include</u> Attorneys, CPA's, Realtors, Bankers, Insurance Representatives, Speakers, Authors, Coaches, Restaurant Owners, Inventors, Trainers, Dentists, Financial Planners, and Doctors to name a few.

From 1993 to 2009, I alone generated 64% of new jobs. That's approximately 10 million jobs for 10 million hard-working Americans. Hey Corporate America, I bet you can't say the same.

Mad Ads is written for me!

Books like this make me smarter, more capable, and ultimately self-reliant. I'm going to grow every day. Not in size, but in profits!

America's Small Business Owner

David T. Fagan & Aaron Halderman

Introduction: Mad Ads and the Mad Men Who Started It All

"Let your mind start a journey through a strange new world. Leave all thoughts of the world you knew before. Let your soul take you where you long to be...Close your eyes, let your spirit start to soar, and you'll live as you've never lived before." – Erich Fromm, German psychoanalyst

It was a clear, crisp day with the scent of fall sneaking past the exhaust fumes and mass human exodus heading for the lunch carts set up on Manhattan street corners. Peeking out between the high-rise spires of stately brownstones and modern glass edifices, a perfect sky of soft denim blue studded with wispy clouds illuminated cabs and buses, bicyclists and purposeful pedestrians striding across the stained sidewalk.

A gull swirled lazily in the air, buoyed by the jet stream, its beady eyes on the lookout for sandwich crumbs and cookie morsels. Suddenly, it took a U-turn, dipping quickly down to the waters off Manhattan. It emerged just seconds later, the silvery, pale indigo scales of a bluefish clamped between the gull's jaws. The bird headed for the well-worn planks of a pier jutting out into the massive expanse of diamond-studded whitecaps surrounding the island. Startled by a gaggle of small children touring the docks, the gull took its precious cargo and headed inland.

As the bird zoomed in on downtown Manhattan, it zoomed perilously near the broad expanse of plate glass windows in a high-rise building crowned by the Met Life logo. Although the floor-to-ceiling windows were painstakingly cleaned and scraped weekly, it didn't take long for the soot and debris of the city to cling to the panes. Nonetheless, the view from Dan Madden's office was spectacular. As the gull flapped by, it was so close that Dan could see the reflection of his building's steel supports in the bird's round black eyes. He took a step backward, startled.

Inside Dan's office, the sounds and smells and hustle and bustle of busy New Yorkers were muted to an almost imperceptible backdrop. His spit-shined leather oxfords clipped noiselessly across the thickly cushioned, short-pile carpet as he turned to the cut-glass decanter atop a blonde wood credenza with spiky metal legs. A mirrored tray held his favorite libation for feeding the muse: Scotch. One cube from the sterling bucket of ice clinked into the bottom of a short, stout rocks tumbler cradled in his hand, followed by a healthy pour from the cut glass decanter.

Dan took the drink with him as he regained his seat behind a modern mahogany desk flanked by a pair of brown suede armchairs. He reached for the golden case engraved with his initials and snapped it open, extracting a cigarette. He held it up to his lips while his free hand grasped a slim Zippo lighter, also engraved with his monogram. A quick flick of flame later and he was gratefully inhaling a long drag of tobacco smoke between his lips while running a hand across his dark hair, held in place with a liberal application of Brylcreem.

Dan's eyes were drawn to the easel in an unobtrusive corner of the office. It held a large piece of tissue paper with a hastily sketched picture of an airplane and a crew of five lined up in front of it, all dressed in uniforms reminiscent of the armed forces. Even the stewardess wore a short-brimmed cap that would appear right at home on Hitler. The copy wasn't much better, some drivel about safety and security when flying on a new commercial airline's 707.

Dan's thoughts wandered in and out, much like the wispy tendrils of smoke passing between his lips only to be sucked back into his lungs. The snowy gull, with its prize of vibrant blue fish. The fiery lemon ball of sun, at its zenith and fleetingly visible between the umpteen-story buildings crowded along the street. As the scotch slid butter-like down Dan's throat he swiveled his chair toward the window and looked down at the busy street scene below. Women in bright red coats and blue-feathered hats mingled amidst a group of businessmen in gray suits brightened by ties of every hue: cerulean, jade, navy, crimson.

Suddenly, Dan turned back to his desk and pulled a pad of paper from the middle drawer. He began furiously writing down phrases, stabbing his ballpoint pen into the page. Although he wasn't an artist, he sketched a quick design on the sheet beneath and made notes in the margin about what colors needed to go where and how to flesh out the ideas.

An hour later, Dan rushed to the art department on the floor below, waving the pad of paper with its scribblings in one hand. "Charley! Draw this up!"

By the time his meeting with the owner of the airline was scheduled the next day, Dan had a complete set of storyboards ready in the conference room. His secretary brought in platters of ripe fruit and aged cheese, along with fresh shrimp cocktails and, of course, full decanters of scotch, rye, and bourbon. He finished lighting a cigarette just as the clients were escorted to the conference room.

"Gentlemen," Dan greeted them, flicking the ashes from his cigarette into a small crystal dish at his elbow, "Settle in and get ready for an advertising campaign that will bring you more business than you can handle."

The clients settled in for libations and smokes while Dan made his presentation. The first storyboard showed the airline crew dressed in fashionable, multi-hued uniforms. The stewardesses, each one svelte and lovely, wore short skirts showing off their fantastic legs along with futuristic-looking bubble helmets atop their perfectly coiffed heads. The next storyboard displayed a fleet of airplanes, each one painted a different, vibrant hue and embellished with a more colorful version of the company logo. The last board pulled all the components together, showing the smiling crew in their eye-catching uniforms dancing in front of a bright blue airplane. The tag line in a large, block font at the top read, "The End of Plain Planes."

Dan's advertising campaign presentation to the airline client was pure brilliance. The airline client signed on the dotted line and the agency celebrated well into the wee hours of the morning at a popular nightclub.

***

This is a fictional story, but it's based on the real-life scenario of a late 1950s and early 1960s era Madison Avenue advertising executive, referred to by the self-coined term of Mad Man. The actual client was Braniff International and their new, post-war slogan, "The End of Plain Planes", was created by real advertising agency Jack Tinker and Partners.

The creative concept for Braniff International was an instant success. World War II was over and, following on its heels, the Korean War was also a thing of the past. Americans were tired of tightening their belts and being bombarded by horrifying news.

Khaki and olive drab were the distasteful symbols of previous austerity. On the verge of a new decade, consumers were ready to usher in a new era of wealth, leisure, and good times. Where once air travel was reserved mainly for military units and the transportation of necessary goods and supplies, the new role of airlines was to whisk Americans away to vacations in exotic destinations around the world. How better to portray an airline remarketing itself for leisure travel than to focus on beauty and visual stimulation?

Back in those days, Braniff International was a multi-million dollar account. Advertising executives like the fictional Dan Madden weren't usually involved in writing the copy or making the drawings, but they were tasked with developing the overall concept of the advertising campaign for the agency's biggest clients. Not only that, the ad exec's job involved schmoozing the clients – wining and dining them in five-star restaurants – in order to persuade them to let go of a large chunk of their hefty bank accounts.

Of course things are far different today – or are they? Those big advertising agencies still have their offices on Madison Avenue and in Manhattan, they still wine and dine their biggest clients, and they still charge an arm and a leg for large-scale advertising campaigns designed to saturate the market with prime-time television and splashy, four-color magazine ads. Nobody smokes in their office anymore and women have now been allowed into the "boys club", but other than that, it's quite surprising how closely a scene from half a century ago relates to the way advertising is done today.

If this is still your concept of what advertising for your business is supposed to be like, get ready for a change in direction, to a place where Madison Avenue meets Main Street, USA.

After stints filling the role of CEO for Jay Conrad Levinson's Guerrilla Marketing brand and Business Development Coach for Infusionsoft, I'm here to bring you a fresh set of inexpensive ideas to make your business get noticed, fast. I'm not the fictional Dan Madden, but I have spent my share of time marketing to big companies and producing creative concepts to drive their advertising to new heights. Mad Ads expands on my Law of Multiplication concept, which allows your business to be everywhere, even though you, as the owner or an executive manager, can't.

No one is in business to get smaller, right? Nor do entrepreneurs wish to stagnate. The idea is to grow. That's why you need big Madison Avenue advertising on a small Main Street budget.

Small business owners need big advertising to compete in any economy, but particularly a recessionary one. In fact as the economy changes, your goals tend to change right along with it. Those lofty objectives identified during the good times might need to take a U-turn and be reduced to simply staying in business. That's a new, but well-trodden path paved with thrift and frustration. I've been in the same place before, and so have millions of other entrepreneurs.

Consumers' needs change, too, in response to what the economy is doing. As I related in the story of Braniff Airlines' advertising campaign, it was successful because the ad execs recognized the mood of the post-war American.

I've spent years consulting with, speaking to, and marketing for a wide variety of clients. Through this experience, I've come to realize there is a dearth of creative advertising information available to small business owners. They've all been led to believe the only effective marketing comes from those fancy, high-end advertising agencies in New York City or Los Angeles. My intent is to fill that gap with a focus on inexpensive, or even free, forms of advertising that any entrepreneur – no matter their marketing budget or lack thereof – can do with a great degree of success.

In a depressed economy, it's not time to stop advertising; it's time to use the law of multiplication and spread your marketing message as effortlessly, quickly, and inexpensively as possible. It's time to target what today's consumers want, and need.

In fact, the economy in recent years has been so bad that many firms, both large and small, have cut back on their marketing budgets drastically. Declining sales don't justify an increase of spending on advertising. This makes sense, to some extent. You can't spend money you don't have (unless you're the government!).

Then again, by pulling back from the market, you are doing your business a disservice. How can you possibly stand out in the forefront of consumers' minds if your advertising is nonexistent? Competition is more fierce than ever as those companies that still have some credit left go full speed ahead vying for the consumer's dollars. I'll go out on a limb and say that exactly the opposite of cutting back is necessary; increased advertising is the way to stay in business, especially in an economic downturn. Fortunately, it doesn't have to cost a lot.

This book is not for big business owners. It's not for large corporations with enough resources to cover temporary setbacks and big in-house agencies with grand marketing ideas. Instead, the readers I want to influence are boot-strap entrepreneurs; savvy businesspeople who don't have the same type of capital funding or financial assets to compete with the big guys; home-based business owners who don't have access to a professional advertising agency or even a fancy office; start-ups who manage a handful of staff and rely on guerrilla tactics to get ahead.

So, what is "big" advertising? My definition is anything that makes a big impact, whether it reaches a huge percentage of your target market, gets a loud buzz going, or results in a hefty return on your investment. I have never seen a direct correlation between the amount of money you spend on a particular advertising campaign and its return. Big Madison Avenue-style advertising is possible with very little money; big success can come with a focus on the goal of increased profitability.

Because of this, you will find that I did not include any type of TV advertising in this book. Television ads are usually far outside the small business owner's marketing budget. Sure, you could run an ad on a public access station or perhaps afford a spot with a local TV station during the wee hours of the morning, but these are not effective ways to spend your advertising dollars. Unless your budget can handle a spot during peak viewing hours for your target audience, television just doesn't provide a good ROI. Instead, this book focuses on the myriad other forms of advertising – 107 to be exact – that utilize much more affordable forms of media and placement. In the chapter on print advertising and specifically magazine ads, for instance, I recommend that you stick

Did you know? A 30-second ad during Fox TV's American Idol costs approximately $750,000.

30-second spot during the 2010 Super Bowl: $2.6 million

with smaller, specialized publications over national magazines claiming huge subscriberships. It's not that a full-page in a glossy issue wouldn't be effective, but for most entrepreneurs the cost is out of reach.

As you read through this book I encourage you to take notes when something resonates and realize how you can use these techniques in the best interests of your own business. I provide examples of actual campaigns defining those moments that changed advertising forever but they are meant merely as references; I always want you to think how you can learn from these examples and tweak the concept to fit perfectly with your products or services and your Main Street budget.

In 2008, the food industry alone spent $32 billion; the auto industry spent $15 billion.

We'll begin by looking at a few key concepts of marketing plans and advertising campaigns so you are prepared, both mentally and financially, to implement the Law of Multiplication. Then we'll dig into the real meat – the actual advertising you can do today to get big results tomorrow!

The various types of marketing are divided into seven categories: Online, Signage, Branding & Promotion, Print, Direct Marketing, People Connections, and Creative Extras. There is a chapter devoted to each that includes a detailed explanation and all the information you need to make the methodology work for you. While the section on Online Advertising is a long one, internet marketing is by no means the only or even the best way to advertise your business. Strive for a well-rounded approach that implements a few ideas from each category to realize the deepest reach into your target market.

Let's move on to the key concepts behind creating a marketing plan you can use to put all the pieces in place.

Chapter One: Every Journey Starts with a Road Map

"Great ideas need landing gear as well as wings." – C.D. Jackson, military adviser to President Eisenhower

Creative ideas and stories about the defining moments of advertising are meant to stimulate your thought processes – and there are lots of those in the upcoming pages. As you read through them, your creative juices are going to flow and you'll be excited to start implementing a new advertising campaign right away. But in order to tie together all of your ideas and then track ROI, you really need to start with a marketing plan. Putting it on paper gives you set goals along with a visual road map of how to proceed.

Caution: along with a plan, you must make a commitment to your marketing; although most of the methods I include in the following chapters are designed to work quickly, the best techniques get better over time.

You don't have to vow 'til death do us part, but you do have to establish a committed relationship with your marketing plan.

The big guys base their advertising on brand building. Who doesn't see the golden arches and immediately think "McDonald's" – even without any further cues? That's due to the intensive branding of the advertising agency they use – and it took decades to develop.

Of course, the advertising in this book is meant to promote your brand, but it is not based on a thirty-year plan. I understand you are a small business owner concerned with the next month or year of sales figures – maybe even next week's!

So let's consider the main components and primary focus of any small business marketing plan. These are Goals & Objectives, Target Market, Methodology, and Budget. Although it's not included as an actual part of the marketing plan, results tracked from each campaign in the current year should be included in the subsequent year's document. If you don't have a way to tell what's working and what isn't, how can your advertising focus on the most successful campaigns? We'll cover the specifics of tracking results in Chapter Three but for now I want you to think about the possibilities as you formulate your plan.

Goals & Objectives

Why should you advertise your business at all? The simple answer is to increase sales, right? As a goal, that's pretty broad. Not only that, it doesn't consider profitability. Doubling your sales doesn't necessarily make your company more profitable, particularly if you are selling more "loss leader" products or services. So the real goal of your advertising is to *increase profits*. When you examine the ROI of your advertising, it functions as a tool for analysis and comparison, not a gauge for the effectiveness of your campaign based solely on sales because *sales are not the goal.* You could realize an awesome response rate to a mailer if you give away something for free but that doesn't add to your bottom line.

Sample Objectives

Convince prospects that our software will help them streamline business processes and now is the best time to buy.

Achieve 50% brand recognition with target market as defined by the consumer's ability to 1) identify our logo; 2) describe our products; and 3) associate quality with our brand.

Achieve 2% response rate and profits of $500 per 100 mailers within one month.

Still, "profitability" is not a realistically manageable or attainable goal. Consider where you want your business to be in the next twelve months. Do you want to hire a manager so you can spend more time away from the office? Do you want to pay for new equipment or your child's college education? When you think of specific goals, you can attach a specific number to their completion. In the first case, perhaps you need to achieve an increase in profits by $36,000 per year in order to cover the costs of adding human resources. A similar amount may be needed to acquire new capital or put your daughter through an undergraduate program. Now you have a goal that you can break down into monthly chunks, annual quarters, and a way to monitor your progress.

What about your business objectives? These are not the same as your goals. Objectives refer to your place in the market; your business niche. Objectives can be described as "To become the widget manufacturer recognized in the tri-state area for exceptional quality" or "To achieve the highest customer satisfaction ratings among widget manufacturers in the nation". Objectives are based on your company's mission statement and align with the goals you have set. The more succinct you can make these objectives, the clearer your vision.

Let's say you own ABC Widget Company and your goal is to hire a facilities manager. You believe the quality of your widgets is exceptional and if you portray that element in your advertising, you are confident sales will increase and you can reach your goal of adding $36,000 in profits by year's end. So your objective is the one stated above, to become recognized by your target market as providing the best quality widgets. Try to reduce that lengthy statement to just a few words: "Widgets that keep your thingama-jigs running". That's a nice, shortened, understandable version that you can tell anyone at any time.

Now you know where you're headed with your advertising and marketing!

Target Market

Thoroughly researching your target market is perhaps the most important part of developing your marketing plan. Your objective should have helped you define your particular industry niche (in the example above, the supplier of the best quality widgets); now you need to define who will utilize it.

There's no short cut to defining your target market. It takes research. According to British advertising great, David Ogilvy, "Advertising people who ignore research are as dangerous as generals who ignore decodes of enemy signals." When you hire a Madison Avenue advertising firm, that's part of the package. When you're a Main Street entrepreneur, it's up to you to do the legwork.

An integral part of that research includes investigation of your typical clients' demographics and psychographics. Those are the terms the big ad execs use so let's break them down.

Demographics are the common characteristics of those consumers who are most likely to purchase your products or services. Demographics can include a wide swath of characteristics such as age, income, education, status, occupation, geographical location, and size of household. Narrower demographics might focus on the age of children in the household, home ownership status, home value, and a geographical location that is urban or rural.

Psychographics are more detailed and include the characteristics of people's lifestyles and behavioral patterns. Psychographics may focus on such factors as where a person prefers to vacation; interests and hobbies; religious and political views; morals, values, and standards.

Defining your target market begins with defining the personal traits, characteristics, and behaviors of people.

But how do you get this information cheaply? One way is to examine your current customer records. Who is your average client right now?

When you need information, usually all you have to do is ask. Go through your customer list and call them, send them an email with a short survey, or mail a postcard giving them access to an anonymous online survey. Generally you will get a better response rate if you can do this face-to-face, during a sales appointment, for instance.

If these methods don't result in a good response rate to your survey, add an incentive for completion such as a freebie, discount, or even cash. It doesn't need to be anything expensive; even enclosing a single dollar bill in an envelope with a printed survey can dramatically increase response rate. It comes down to the concept of reciprocity. When you give something away for free, a person feels much more inclined to reciprocate – an important concept to remember as you develop your marketing plan.

In addition to a survey sent to your current clientele, you can research your target market in the following easy, inexpensive ways:

- Slip in a pre-stamped customer satisfaction survey with each fulfilled order.

- Examine past sales records of shipping addresses, items purchased, subsequent sales, etc. by customer. Look for trends.

  o If you have time, call this list of former customers and find out why they buy from you or are no longer doing business with your company.

- Even better, make an appointment with each of your current clients. Spend some time chatting and getting to know them better. This is a great way to casually question your customers and help you define your target market.

- Research the broad demographics of your clients' geographic area. If your business markets mostly to local patrons, visit your Chamber of Commerce and ask for compiled statistics on area businesses and residents.

- Use an opt-in form on your website or mail a business reply card to inquirers. Ask for information such as birth date, household size, children's ages, etc. (this also builds your database).

- Print a warranty card to be included with each purchase; make it necessary for the consumer to mail it in to activate the warranty period. Include questions regarding demographics.

- Data mine through your website. Use statistics from website visitors to add to your research. Most tracking software – even free versions – provide a wealth of statistics such as

- o Geographic location (City, State, Country)
- o Internet service provider
- o Search keywords
- o Referral URL
- o Search engine (and country of origin)
- o Most popular pages
- o Entry/exit pages

These research methods give you a good idea of what type of customer you currently service, but what if your business levels are stagnating or declining? This would be a good time to target a new segment of clients. Consider expanding your reach to consumers who are emerging as some of the fastest growing markets. These include women, senior citizens, ethnic groups, and home-based business owners. There are plenty of other under-served markets, too, such as the hearing or visually impaired, gay couples, the physically handicapped, young (under age 25) entrepreneurs, environmental activists or green consumers, older parents…the list goes on and on. Think outside the box to find a new target market that might have need of your products or services, and then learn the techniques and communication methods necessary to contact these demographics in an effective manner.

Now add your identified niche (your unique offering) and target market (your unique customers) demographics research into your overall marketing strategy. As we proceed with methodology, keep in mind the triggers that will appeal to these consumers. Remember, the purpose of your marketing plan is to maximize profits – not just attain more sales. Steady profits come from creativity, adherence to the plan, and attention to the ultimate goal – the long-term vision for the future of your company. That long-term vision is a focus on reaching the maximum number of prospects for the maximum amount of profit.

Methodology

Your research on the demographics and psychographics of your target market provides valuable information that will guide the type, media, content, and placement of your advertising. Put those statistics to work by creating the right message for the right market at the right time. Easier said than done, I know. But the "how" can be figured out if you first consider the "who", "what", and "where". You already know who you're marketing to based on your research, but how about the "what" and "where"?

Think about what you want to offer based on what you know about your target market. What is going to appeal to them most? It might be a discount coupon, a testimonial from someone famous, a validation of superior quality, or a demonstration of your product's practical uses. The point is that it should appeal specifically to what's most important to those people who make up the majority of your customer base. Show them very explicitly *what's in it for them*.

A technique that may help you get a better idea of what your target market is seeking in a product or service is the development of a "passenger story". If you were taking a drive with a prospective client sitting in the passenger seat, what would you tell them about your business?

Put yourself in the shoes of your customer for a moment. Imagine a day in the life; the hurdles and obstacles you encounter as well as those things that could make your life easier. What makes you fearful? What makes you happy? What stresses you out? Think of your main concerns.

Work backwards from your position as the seller. Start thinking about advertising from the perspective of your customer. When you've gotten inside the head of your customer, imagine what might make you buy; consider what type of story would be appealing and personally targeted.

For instance, let's imagine that the largest portion of the customer database at ABC Widget Company is comprised of small manufacturing firms headed by a middle-aged male with a minimum wage staff. What is this person's typical day going to be like? Chances are he runs the business as a way to support his family. He doesn't make big profits. He's probably worried about how he's going to pay for capital expenses and whether or not his employees will leave him for a better position elsewhere. Base your passenger story on: 1) ABC Widgets is a small company, too, with the same problems; 2) You offer a payment plan to make your products affordable; and 3) The quality of ABC's widgets is superior, equaling less frustration and less down time for line workers.

Your passenger story is a real-life example. It shows potential clients that you identify with them (based on your research) and presents a scenario that clearly illustrates you are a partner in solving one of their problems, making their life easier, or providing a really cool form of entertainment. Your product or service is going to make their lives better – so much better that they can't help but overcome any objections and open their checkbooks. *Remove any emotional barriers.*

Something else to consider at this point is the current perception of your product or service – is it negative? Then you've got a lot to overcome in removing buying barriers, but it's not impossible. Think about the story included in the introduction. Back in those days when Mad Men ruled the advertising industry, people smoked all the time, anywhere. In the early 1960s, however, the Surgeon General released an official report of the detrimental effects of cigarettes. All of a sudden tobacco companies and their advertising agencies were in a tailspin. How do you overcome such a negative report and the resultant restrictions on cigarette advertisements? The majority of tobacco companies started offering and marketing "light" cigarettes with less tar and nicotine. These types of advertisements were meant to change the consumer's negative perception of a product they'd been told was harmful. *Great advertising changes perception.*

The Little Bug That Could

The year was 1934. Adolph Hitler and his Third Reich ruled Germany with an iron fist. But one thing Hitler wanted to provide for his people was a car affordable to anyone. He approached the Porsche company with the design requirements of a vehicle that got excellent fuel mileage, could seat two adults and three children and be priced well below any other autos on the market. A prototype was developed and dubbed Volkswagen, literally the "car of the people". By 1936, the first version of the Beetle was zooming (at a top speed of 65 mph) along Germany's Autobahn.

After several setbacks which included finding a new manufacturer and work force, and a little event called World War II, Hitler put the project on hold. After Hitler's suicide and the end of the war, Germany needed to rebuild itself. The Volkswagen went back into production.

The Beetle was popular in Europe but not so much in America. In fact, Volkswagen, being a product of Germany and the brainchild of Hitler, was extremely unpopular. How, then, could an advertising agency turn such a huge negative into a positive?

The New York agency of Doyle Dane Bernbach managed to do it. With tongue-in-cheek copy, they emphasized those qualities of the

Beetle that were barriers to sales. For instance, one ad showed a picture of the bug with a single word below it, "Lemon". The negative connotation was turned around by the copy, which stated the quality standards of Volkswagen were so high that this particular car was rejected because of a blemish on the dash. Billboards were erected with such great copy as "Think Small" and "We'll Never Make it Big".

The advertising campaign worked exceptionally well. All of a sudden the Beetle was cute. It got great gas mileage. As the 1960s wore on and hippies vowed to make peace, not war, the Volkswagen bug became the popular anti-establishment, anti-materialism symbol of a generation.

For this reason, the campaign of Doyle Dane Bernbach for Volkswagen Beetle was a defining moment in the history of advertising. The agency managed to accomplish what most people thought of as impossible – and did it so skillfully it became one of the best-selling cars of all time.

Your advertising offer also needs to be in line with the purpose of your marketing. What specific action do you want someone to take when they encounter your advertisements? Should they opt-in to your website, give your office a call to make an appointment, or return a business reply card asking for further information? This helps narrow down the methodology of your advertising and focuses it on the real purpose and goal.

Where can you find your target market? How you advertise will depend largely on where potential customers tend to hang out. Are they young? You'll likely find them online the majority of the time. Are they homemakers? Then the grocery store would be a good place for your ads. Is yours a B2B company? Business associations and trade periodicals might be your best bet.

We can take this concept one step further. *Target audience advertising* refers to placing ads in front of an audience that is already interested in some aspect related to your product or service. This is most often seen on television, in magazines, and during live events. For example, during a TV show such as AMC's *Mad Men*, which takes place in the early '60s, you are likely to see ads associated with products of that era; they are also likely to use a retro theme. A recent spot for Clorox bleach featured a crisp white shirt with a lipstick stain on the collar and a tag line of "Getting ad guys out of hot water for generations". At an MLB baseball game, you might see the jumbo-tron air an ad for Ball Park franks. During a music awards show, the commercials are bound to feature the places where consumers can download the award-winning songs and buy the CDs. Pay attention next time you are viewing a special event or TV show and you'll begin to realize just how effectively the big companies target a specific audience.

Right now I just want you to start thinking about the various types of advertising that will best target the consumers interested in your products or services, but not commit to anything. Future chapters provide over a hundred different methods, so by the end of this book you'll have a better idea of which forms of advertising you will want to try. Then you can place them in your marketing plan. The more methods you utilize, the greater your chances of success with one or more; in fact, the effect is both multiplicative and synergistic.

Global advertising dollars are expected to reach $544 billion in 2010

Budget

Now comes the not-so-fun part: putting numbers into the marketing plan and assigning dollar amounts based on a percentage of revenue to each marketing method.

This takes some careful consideration. Most small business owners allocate just four percent of total sales to advertising. But consider this: if you commit to spending up to ten or even twelve and a half percent this year and the same dollar amount in subsequent years, this expenditure decreases as a ratio to increasing sales, adding more profitability to your bottom line. That initial benchmark gets built upon every year, increasing brand awareness and market reach, providing a solid foundation for success while costing less and less. Pretty nifty!

Take into consideration your time, too. You may find a really effective form of marketing that is free but if it takes you four hours to develop it, that's part of your budget. Those four hours weren't used in a direct sales activity (green time). Even though it's an important activity, there is an associated cost.

Allocating a double digit percentage of your sales to the marketing budget can be a bit frightening. But remember that it is an investment and a commitment. You have to stick to the plan (although not so rigidly that you don't give up on what's not working) to reap the benefits. Think of it this way: if you have a bad month and decide to take your marketing budget down to zero, will it save you money? It might be one less expenditure but it's not going to increase your bottom line. Advertising, on the other hand, *can* do that.

Money spent on advertising isn't dollars that could be used to buy new equipment; it's an investment in your business and its profitability. Sure, a modern widget manufacturing machine might reduce the costs of production but it isn't going to bring a new customer through the door. Again, advertising *can* do that.

For the thrifty entrepreneur, there are many ways to reduce the cost of marketing. Two of the most common methods are cooperative advertising (where an industry partner such as a franchiser or manufacturer shares the cost) and joint ventures (a complementary company advertises with you). But there are a lot more ways to make it affordable. Why not barter something you can provide in exchange for a newspaper or radio ad? You can exchange links with another company online; you can also exchange ad space or promo opportunities offline. Enlist your kids' help – give them a stack of business cards or brochures and pay them a quarter for every one they hand out to adults at a school sports game or concert. Don't forget family members and friends and their connections, too. Chances are they are more than willing to help you succeed.

A marketing plan isn't a static document; it's a working tool. Once you've got the elements of Goals & Objectives, Target Market, Methodology, and Budget in your marketing plan, then you have a road map for your company's journey to success. It doesn't mean you can't stray from the defined path. Its purpose is to maintain your focus and keep your vision at the forefront of everything you do to advertise your business.

Chapter Two: Creative Advertising – The Seduction of the Customer

"The problem is never how to get new, innovative thoughts into your mind, but how to get old ones out. Every mind is a building filled with archaic furniture. Clean out a corner of your mind and creativity will instantly fill it." – Dee Hock, founder & former CEO of Visa

If your marketing plan is the road map to success, think of advertising methodology as the fun stops along the journey: an ice cream parlor for an afternoon break, the museum filled with odd and unusual curiosities, the national park with majestic vistas. Adding guerrilla creativity to all of your advertising ensures that any travelers along the same route will want to take the time for a pit stop.

This doesn't mean that your marketing needs to be whacky or over-the-top. You are not vying for this year's Clio advertising award. Remember the whole purpose of your advertisements is to increase profits. Creativity only has value as it relates to this goal – and it should be a fun process to inject your advertising with fresh and innovative themes.

Focus on the Familiar

Do you recall the exercise I asked you to perform in the last chapter? The one about putting yourself inside your customer's head to develop your passenger story? Leo Burnett, the late advertising executive and owner of the agency where Jay Conrad Levinson collaborated on such famous campaigns as the Jolly Green Giant and the Marlboro Man, explains successful marketing this way, "The secret of all effective originality in advertising is not the creation of new and tricky words and pictures, but one of putting familiar words and pictures into new relationships." Obviously he and his agency did that quite effectively.

Connecting a familiar feeling with the attribute of a product is also referred to as experience advertising. For instance, the Marlboro Man associated the freedom of a cowboy on the range with smoking a Marlboro cigarette. The Jolly Green Giant was aimed at kids, showing them how they, too, could grow up big and strong by eating their veggies. Morris the Cat and his curmudgeon personality perfectly conveyed how a big, old cat might feel about his daily bowl of food. These are all experiences everyone is familiar with; they are personified by a character that came to be

The Clio Awards have been around since 1959. They were named after the Greek muse.

Leo Burnett and David Ogilvy are both past winners.

irrevocably associated with a product – even today, decades after the last commercial aired.

Back in the heyday of Mad Men, this might have included a political statement. For instance, the cover of *Esquire Magazine* in the 1960s was usually quite controversial. It featured such images as Sonny Liston portrayed as the first Black Santa, a woman applying a razor to her shaving creamed cheeks (Entitled "Why Can't a Woman be More Like a Man?), and other controversial topics regarding the war, domestic violence, and sexuality. Arguably, no other magazine since has taken such risks, and got so many people talking. For the small business owner, I can't recommend this. Yes, it makes for a memorable, buzz-worthy ad, but it can also be very offensive and a Main Street entrepreneur can't afford the negative publicity. A better risk to take is being *authentic*.

Your advertisements need to correlate with what customers already find familiar. It's your creative twist, however, that makes the subject matter stand out by portraying the specific benefit or purpose of your company's offerings.

And no matter how creative, the ads need to uphold the goals and objectives of your organization while portraying its unique "personality". People don't buy from companies; they buy from people. People don't buy based on what an agency tells them to buy; they buy based on the evocation of feelings and experiences associated with a brand.

Make Them Pay Attention; Make Them Act

This is where your passenger story comes into play. Consumers are only interested in something that appeals to them personally. If it doesn't, you'll soon find the person sitting in the passenger seat turning up the radio to drown you out. Because your passenger story is based on a real-life scenario, it speaks directly to your target market's interests – and it is memorable. The advertisements you create include a specific call to action; the purpose of the ads. When these two elements – a memorable story and a call to action – are combined, they make for a very powerful form of marketing.

Let's consider the call to action. When you ask someone to take a specific action, you first must remove the physical, emotional, and financial objections that would prevent them from acting. It takes more than just repeating your phone number to make someone call. What's going to happen when a potential customer calls? What's in it for them? Provide a toll-free number and ensure that someone knows the real and tangible reasons why they *need* to call. The easier and faster you make the expected response, the more you can expect your call to action will be heeded.

And the more specific you can make your message, the better it will perform. Let me give you another way of looking at this. Your advertising is meant to reach the most people possible. But no matter what message and what method you use, you are never going to reach only those who might be interested in your product or service. Some people just aren't going to be interested. So do you develop an ad campaign that is really broad and hopes to catch a few interested parties in a wide net? Or do you specifically target the ideal buyer who might represent a small portion of those who see your advertisement?

The second scenario is more viable. If your ad speaks directly to one person in a hundred and that one person buys your product today, then it's a success. The other 99 are irrelevant. In fact, you could even consider how to write an ad that *eliminates* the 99 consumers who are unlikely to become buyers because they can't afford your offerings, they're not in the market for your services, or they aren't loyal to a brand.

You may have heard some Mad Men refer to ads as "sexy". They're not talking about massage oil; they're referring to the power of an ad to seduce your prospective customer. The copy wiggles its way into the mind, breaks down emotional barriers, and sweeps past objections to turn a prospect into a buyer.

This is the psychological element of truly innovative marketing. Consumers need to understand the benefits of buying a particular product or service from your company – and only your company. Ensure they comprehend the value proposition. Identify the buying trigger – that one factor that erases any objections –

based on your target market research. Tell them plainly that you can provide exactly what they need or want. Speak to their emotions. Seduce them.

Seduction can occur as either a conscious or subconscious advertising element; that is, it can manifest as a tangible benefit or an emotional trigger. The tangible benefit modifies behavior while the emotional trigger changes attitude. The best advertising addresses both needs. You need the smoldering coals to cook along with the meat to satisfy the appetite; seductive pop and sizzle and the scent of beef without putting a hamburger on the grill doesn't provide any satisfaction. When your product or service is portrayed as doing something beneficial while making the buyer feel good you've got a real win on your hands. Tantalize the taste buds then provide the meat.

Pump Up Your Creative Muscle

These are the elements of good advertising but how can you make it creative? Some people have a hard time with this. They are so familiar with their company's offerings that it becomes difficult to think of them in new and attractive ways.

Creativity is talent that becomes more developed through exercise. Just like a bicep you want to pump up, your creative juices can be induced to flow. Some ways to hone your imagination include reading about current events online, perusing your compe-

Are You Creative?
Does this describe you:

Your taste in music and art is "eclectic"

You have hundreds of stories in your head

You enjoy learning new words

Inspiration is the solution to your problems

tition's promotional materials, finding the most popular trending topics on Twitter, joining a local business networking group, or browsing through newspapers and magazines. The more you know about what's going on, the more effectively your advertising can tap into that popularity – and the prevailing sentiment of today's consumer.

For instance, when the real estate market took a steep dive, it produced a huge entrepreneurial interest in loan modification companies, rental units, and legal representation during foreclosure proceedings. Those companies that paid attention to the trend and capitalized on it not only survived, but thrived.

Keep your company's objectives and message in mind as you look through various forms of media; this should help stimulate your creativity while inspiring you to use the general ideas of others and personalize them for your business. There's no need to reinvent the wheel – but your advertising does need to look different from other company's.

Another way to add creativity to your advertising campaign is to combine elements. Those tangibles and intangibles we discussed make the perfect combination. Take an intangible, such as high customer satisfaction ratings, and add it to a tangible, such as the usefulness of your product. The intangible may be portrayed by an image you use in your advertisements, perhaps a group of smiling people (think of Verizon and how they used pictures of a big network of people to indicate they stand behind their products). Or consider the example given earlier of the Jolly Green Giant. This easily recognizable figure became an icon of the company and appealed not only to kids, but to moms who wanted to serve nutritious vegetables to their families. The big green guy was the tangible image that portrayed that feeling of satisfaction (and it became ever more clear when the advertising team added "Little Sprout"). Your advertising copy should focus on the tangible benefit with an image relevant to the overall message. Ensure the two elements are something with which most people (or at least your target market) identify.

The Jolly Green Giant is the third most recognized advertising icon of the 20th century, just behind Ronald McDonald and the Marlboro Man

Do tie the elements in with the overall message and objective of your advertising. Measure it against your marketing plan's goal – does it fit?

Mix It Up

Mixed methodology is also very effective. Even if you run an online business, there's no reason to forgo more traditional forms of advertising. The various forms of marketing media can very beautifully work in sync, using a call to action to take offline customers online and vice versa.

Go Daddy Drives Offline Consumers Online

Go Daddy was just an unknown start-up domain registrar and web hosting business when the company decided to spend all of its marketing budget in one fell swoop: an ad during the Super Bowl. Although it had been around since 1997, operating under the name Jomax Technologies, it would not be until 2005 that Go Daddy became a household name and gained a rank in advertising history.

Their in-house advertising team knew the Super Bowl commercial had to be something special. After all, they weren't spending millions of dollars on one spot only to figure out they'd made a mistake in attracting market share. It had to be interesting, edgy, and well, sexy – or as CEO Bob Parsons puts it, "fun, edgy, and a bit inappropriate".

What did the team come up with? They recruited Candice Michelle from the World Wrestling Federation and created a parody of Janet

Jackson's infamous "wardrobe malfunction" which occurred during the previous year's Super Bowl.

The ad appeared a total of one time before Fox pulled it due to the content being deemed inappropriate for family viewers. But it was enough to cause a huge buzz and become one of the most watched spots in Super Bowl history.

Go Daddy was smart enough to take advantage of a tremendous opportunity as it was presented. They uploaded the commercial to their website, where censors couldn't take it down. Since that first year of Super Bowl advertising, Go Daddy now submits a tamer version of the commercial and then drives consumers online to watch the full, unabridged version. This is absolutely brilliant because that is the whole purpose of the ad anyway: to drive traffic online. It's an excellent example of how mixed media can be manipulated to full advantage.

Need some examples of how this can work for your business? Why not advertise on the radio and include your website address? Once the prospective customer visits your website, provide an opt-in form. Then send him or her a mailed catalog or brochure. You could also write a weekly series of blog posts that establish you as an authority on a particular topic. Drive those online readers offline to your business by asking them to call and use a specific discount code to receive a special offer. Sponsor an offline contest but post the results online; require opt-in to view the standings and ultimate winner.

These types of mixed advertising reach your customer in the car, online, at work, and at home. You've easily just quadrupled your reach – using the Law of Multiplication to extend your marketing reach across media platforms.

While we're on the topic of measuring, let's continue on to the final part of any successful advertising campaign: tracking the results of your efforts.

Chapter Three: The Importance of Tracking and Testing, then Testing Some More

"Never stop testing, and your advertising will never stop improving." – David Ogilvy, British advertising executive

I've shared with you several times the importance of committing to your marketing plan. You can't simply send out one mailer, for instance, and expect the phone to start ringing off the hook. You must commit to it, keep it going, build brand recognition. Modern consumers are inundated with advertising from all sides: on the internet, on their cell phone, on the television, on the radio (even satellite radio service airs commercials during syndicated programs), in their mailbox, in their email inbox, on the side of the road, on the side of a bus, in the newspaper, in magazines. No matter where you turn, commercialism is staring you in the face. How can anyone remember an ad they've been exposed to a single time?

65% of consumers think they are constantly bombarded with ads.

In the 1970s, the average city dweller received 1,000 ad messages per day. Today, that number has increased to approximately 5,000.

By the same token, however, neither should you keep pouring money into an ineffective campaign. Although it's been attributed to various famous people, I believe it is Benjamin Franklin who defined insanity as doing the same thing over and over again yet expecting a different result. Some of your marketing just isn't going to work. You might as well realize this now.

With advertising there's a fine line between commitment and insanity. In order to identify that fine line, a system of tracking results is vital. As they say, the numbers don't lie.

The Time Commitment

You really won't have a good idea of how effective any campaign is until it has run for a good three months or more. Repetition is the key to working on the subconscious mind. If you're of a certain age and grew up in a small town, chances are you never heard of Wal-Mart, Pizza Hut, or even McDonald's until years after these brands were well established. Their fame didn't come overnight; it took decades of marketing with some consistency and regularity in order to build the brands.

As the late American novelist Ellen Glasgow said, "The key to everything is patience. You get the chicken by hatching the egg – not by smashing it." You can't hit someone over the head once with your advertising message and expect them to remember it when it comes time to purchase. Bigger doesn't necessarily equate to better; consistency, commitment, and *connecting* are the keys to success. Your competition isn't going to stop marketing and neither should you. But which company will be remembered when it comes time to purchase? The one that made a concerted effort on establishing a real connection over time.

> *Sam Walton was a true guerrilla marketer. He spent 1/3 of the budget of his competitors, trimming his advertising down to 12 campaigns per year. Walton focused on ads that were very targeted to his market and within a few short years, overtook his competitors.*

The Repetition and Consistency Commitment

One of the best ways to increase profitability is not to focus on adding more and more new customers. Rather, your advertising should attract loyal clientele who purchase from your company more than once. It could also concentrate on increasing the amount of the purchase through upsales. Isn't it easier – and cheaper – to send ten widgets a month to one customer than to find ten new customers who each order one widget per month? That's why looking at response rate alone is not a good indicator of success.

Besides this, effective marketing in the Web 2.0 era focuses on establishing relationships rather than diving right into the sales pitch, unlike the Mad Men era when consumers were a captive audience. Today's Americans need never leave their house to do business. They can surf the 'net, email, Skype, instant message, place an online order, fax, or inquire over the phone. How can you possibly establish a relationship with someone you might never meet in person? The answer is, of course, advertising. Repeated and consistent advertising. Even something as simple as requiring your employees to wear a shirt with your logo can have a positive effect on this "ghost" consumer. While your housebound Aunt Mabel is enjoying her soaps on TV one afternoon she might see your delivery van pull up to the neighbor's house and watch as your employees get out and put a new refrigerator on the dolly. Next time Aunt Mabel needs a new appliance, that image just might stick with her and if it does, you can bet she'll be calling your company to make a purchase.

Tracking

How do you track responses from a particular advertising campaign? How do you know that someone called your office in response to a specific advertisement?

In some cases this is really simple. For instance, if you mail a postcard or send an email message advertising a special offer, all you have to do is instruct the recipient to mention a specific code when they place their order. The same holds true for any print ad in a magazine, newsletter, or newspaper. A self-addressed business reply mailer can contain the code on the postcard or envelope that gets returned. That's pretty easy. But what about other forms of advertising?

One way of tracking results from various media is to supply a unique toll-free number or website URL that is used only in conjunction with a particular campaign. If your call to action is asking the prospect to pick up the phone and call your office, this unique number alerts you to which advertisement prompted the action. By the same token, setting up a unique landing page just to track responses to a banner ad provides the same tracking ability. These days both phone numbers and domain names are really cheap, making this method of tracking affordable to any business.

If you are doing other forms of advertising online such as a link exchange, it's easy to see where visitors are coming from via your website's statistics software. I already mentioned this during the section on target market research tactics, but the same software can also be used as a tracker by looking at the "referred from" statistics showing the visitor's path to your site.

And finally, train your sales staff to always ask where a prospect came from when they are communicating with someone for the first time. Keeping track of referrals can be as simple as using a sheet of paper with tick marks but it really provides some valuable information for tracking response rates. Enforce this rule. It will become habit over time.

So we know that marketing success occurs over time and that each campaign needs a unique tracking code. Now it's time to develop a tool that will show actual ROI and response rates. Start with your current baseline profitability before you begin any new campaign and then track response rates (in the form of margin between cost of sales and purchase price) alongside this figure. There are many more metrics that could be analyzed, such as time spent on a web page or return visits, but for the purposes of the small business owner, profitability is still the most important factor. If such variables as brand interaction and number of "mouse overs" are important, there are many software packages, in addition to search engine dashboards, that can provide this type of in-depth analysis.

One of the simplest ways of tracking the effectiveness of your campaigns is with a spreadsheet. When you've got all the methods you are going to use listed in your marketing plan, take that list and add it to a spreadsheet. Include the unique offer code for that promotion, if using.

Each tab on the spreadsheet will represent one month. This allows you to identity seasonal trends, and also clearly portrays specific forms of advertising you use during various times of the year – particularly important for retail businesses. This also lets you accrue funds allocated for each type of marketing (i.e. the cost of a phone book listing divided over a 12-month period).

To each tab, add a column for the total cost, one to track inquiries (or responses) from that particular promotion, another for sales, yet another for profits, and a final column for comments. The comments section helps you remember what went right and what went wrong; what you would change and what you would keep the same in the future. The more comprehensive the comments, the better it will trigger your memory in the future.

Here's an example of a very simplified spreadsheet you can use as a template:

Method	Cost (Monthly)	# of Inquiries	Sales	Profit	Comments
1/4 page ad in Widgets Monthly/Code WM10	$500	10	2	$100	Placement was next to fold on inside page
30 second radio spot/sponsor of local news on KWWW	$400	20	5	$250	Ads ran at the top of each hour, 8 AM to noon
Local Yellow Pages	$30	5	1	$10	Smallest listing without ad space

Online business directory: JonesCounty-Shops.com	$10	1	0	0	County directory

If your business offers a lot of different products or services, you might want to keep a separate spreadsheet that shows the marketing efforts you've used for each category. This is helpful so that you can spot trends. For example, if you are an author of both cookbooks and history texts you can use one parallel advertisement but vary its placement and methodology. Obviously these products are aimed at two different target markets, yet there are similarities. Did a classified ad in a magazine net you greater profitability than a radio ad? Of course, your cookbooks might be advertised in a gourmet foods magazine and your history tomes get a classified in an issue of a military association's quarterly rag. Maybe the cookbooks get a spotlight during a weekly radio cooking show and the history books are advertised during the local station's oldies countdown. When you keep track of the statistics over time, one particular type of media will most likely show a greater ROI over the other.

Tracking results does not have to be particularly scientific, use complicated algorithms, or require a course in statistics. If you use Excel, it's easy to create a pie chart or line graph that charts the results of your advertising campaigns or a pivot chart to drill down on certain elements. This visual representation should be adequate in determining what's working and what's not – and along with the marketing plan, clearly show the course of your marketing journey.

Testing

One question that comes up quite often when clients are speaking to me about their advertising campaigns is how to tell what went wrong. There are so many variables which contribute to a campaign's failure or success. It could be the wrong time of year to advertise certain items; it could be that your mailer was sent to the wrong database; then again it might be the ad itself: the copy, design, colors, images, etc. As the late businessman, John Wanamaker, is quoted as saying, "I know half the money I spend on advertising is wasted, but I can never find out which half." So how can you tell which element contributed to a particular campaign's demise – or even if you should spend money on it in the first place?

It's worth pointing out here that doing a small test run before starting a full-blown campaign is *always cheaper* than the alternative. I can think of many instances where the failure to adequately test beforehand cost a company lots of money in the long run.

Think of such famous flops as the Edsel, New Coke, Betamax, Arch Deluxe burger, and others as prime examples of big Madison Avenue marketing campaigns gone wrong.

What went wrong with the <u>Arch Deluxe?</u>
The "Burger with the grown-up taste" wasn't something the McDonald's target market wanted. It went too far away from what customers have come to expect from McDonald's – cheap and tasty food, not sophisticated fare. The company's biggest value proposition is <u>consistency</u>. Had it been marketed as merely another burger, the Arch Deluxe might still be on the menu today.

One of my clients learned this lesson the hard way. He's an attorney who specializes in helping clients with IRS debt. He decided to branch out after the real estate market bombed and target homeowners facing foreclosure. He developed a direct mail piece to send to a new list of people who had been notified their home was going to auction. Unfortunately, his mailing went out to the wrong database – one comprised of homeowners who had fallen behind on their mortgage payments. You can bet that when they received his letter regarding foreclosure action, these poor homeowners were more than a little surprised and upset. If the attorney had simply tested the letter by sending it out to a handful of addresses on his list first, he would have recognized his mistake much sooner and saved a lot of heartache and angry phone calls!

That's just one example of how you can test a particular advertisement before it reaches the masses. Another method is split testing.

Most often this term is used for internet banner advertising but it really applies to any form of marketing. The idea is to create two similar ads and run them concurrently, but change one element. So, for example, if you are mailing out postcards you might print out two versions; both have the same copy on the address side but you change the graphics on the flip side. If you're the owner of ABC Widget Company, perhaps one postcard shows a smiling customer holding up a widget with a title that says "These widgets are the best." The other postcard has a picture of the manufacturing line working industriously and a blurb of "Only the best people make the best widgets." You split your database in half and send one postcard to each segment then track the response rate to each. It may be that your target market responds better to one photo over the other – but you'll never know unless you split test the piece.

You can apply the same split testing principle to newspaper ads. In most cities, there are several newspapers to choose from, including the small, free classified advertising papers like the Thrifty Nickel or Penny Saver. But which ones are the best to place your advertisement? Try running a different offer in each one. You could put a "buy one get one (BOGO)" offer in the local daily, a coupon for a free upgrade in the Thrifty Nickel, and a 10% discount offer in a weekly publication. This makes each of them easy to track since the offers are so diverse. Try it for a month or two and see which results in the most favorable ROI. That's the one you need to continue using for a daily or weekly ad – and drop all the rest.

The same type of testing is useful for radio advertising, as well. Chances are you've got lots of different stations in your area to choose from. The demographics and psychographics of your target market will give you a good indication of which radio stations are most likely to reach them; for instance, conservatives tend to enjoy talk radio and country music, staunchly religious consumers listen to Christian music, a younger crowd usually tunes into current top 40 hits. If you live in a big city, there may be several choices for each of these programming options. Concurrent ads running on the same days and times with different offers will let you know which stations are most effective.

Testing the response rates of signage is a bit more tricky. You might print several copies of one poster and place it on the bulletin board at the grocery store, the announcements board at the senior center, in store windows, or even pasted to the door of public rest room stalls. How will you know which location is the most effective? The best solution is to ask. Remember that you are training your sale staff to always ask callers where they found out about your company. If someone responds that they saw one of your signs, ask them where it was posted.

When you use tracking codes, be sure to add them to your spreadsheet. If you use different offers, remember to add the specific offer to the comments (or create another column for this information) so you can see which one performed best.

I hope I have convinced you how important tracking and testing are when it comes to advertising on a strict budget. You don't have the marketing dollars McDonald's does and you can't afford a big flop like the Arch Deluxe. Take the time to test each piece (at least any of substantial cost) and then track its results. Without this information you are simply making a stab in the dark hoping your message will stick somewhere – and throwing money away as well. And who can afford to do that?

David T. Fagan & Aaron Halderman

Chapter Four: Internet Marketing – Turn On, Plug In, Make Profits

"More and more marketers are starting to realize that, in a lot of cases, this [internet marketing] should be their first buy. It's easy to do it, it's easy to measure results, it's not that difficult to learn, and there's a low barrier to entry." – Ron Belanger, Yahoo Search Marketing

The 31 forms of online mad ads for the small business owner are:

1. Website
2. Search Engine Optimization (SEO)
3. RSS feeds
4. Video
5. Link exchange
6. Sponsored link
7. Opt-ins
8. Auto responder sequence
9. eBooks
10. Blog
11. Social Bookmarking
12. eBrochure
13. eGreeting cards
14. Game
15. Forum
16. Online Contest
17. Online Survey
18. Podcasts
19. Shopping Cart upsells
20. Social Media
21. Social Groups
22. Viral/Referral Marketing
23. Facebook ads
24. Pay-per-click (PPC)
25. Guest blogging
26. E-zine
27. Article Directories
28. Bulletin/Message Boards
29. Online Business Directories
30. Webinars
31. iPhone/Smart Phone Apps

As we delve into the actual techniques of advertising on a budget, I've started with the category of internet marketing because it is the largest. And so it should be; just as Ron Belanger states this is one of the easiest, cheapest, most effective forms of marketing within the reach of any business owner. The internet is your virtual salesperson that responds to anyone, anywhere, anytime – and never takes a sick day or vacation!

The internet has done a lot of things for our world and the way we live. But perhaps its greatest contribution, at least for small businesses, is that it has leveled the playing field. The owner of ABC Widget Company has the same opportunities to market online as Wal-Mart, McDonald's, and Chevrolet.

Actually, because these giant corporations are so diverse, they can't do the same job of online social marketing you can. If you follow Jack in the Box on Twitter, you know you're not communicating with a real guy who has an antenna ball for a head. Chances are you're just hoping for a coupon code to get a free order of egg rolls. If you're ABC Widget Company, you can tweet about personal activities, industry information, or news and establish a real relationship.

The same marketing principles apply online as well as offline. The best places to advertise are those where your target market is likely to be found – and it varies by industry (based on keyword). For instance, people who are interested in technology (keywords: software, hardware, video games, etc.) are more likely to use search engines to find information and gather on LinkedIn. Those who are avid about entertainment (keywords: movies, books, magazines, restaurants) are apt to talk about it on Facebook and scroll through blog posts. Non-profits overwhelmingly use social media, in particular LinkedIn and YouTube. This is important information to help you determine the best places for your online advertising campaigns. You can't just throw money and energy into an online presence without carefully considering which media will result in the greatest ROI.

Regardless of where your target market hangs out online, you have to establish an online presence and that requires a website first and foremost.

Websites

Social media is just one way to advertise online – and it's a great one. But you have to start with the basics of an online presence and that's a **website**. Every business needs a website. I can't tell you how many Main Street business owners I've encountered in big cities and rural locales alike that refuse to acknowledge the importance of even a single page on the internet. They stubbornly insist that "My customers already know how to get hold of me" or "If they want to buy something, they'll walk into my store." Why would you want to make it so hard? Why wouldn't you want new customers to be able to find you easily and discover what you offer? Are a $10 domain name and a $100 a year hosting service – less than $11 per month – not worth the investment?

Your website is the foundation of your online presence. Whatever type of internet marketing you do – from chats to forums to bulletin boards to blogging – you need a place to direct those virtual contacts. It's highly unlikely that someone who finds information about your company online will rush to the phone and give you a call. Chances are they will, however, visit your website and take a look around. They might even buy something if you make the pages easily navigable, the information comprehensive, and the ordering process convenient.

In June of 1993, there were a total of 130 websites. Four short years later there were nearly three quarters of a million. In 1995 there were one million Internet hosts (host name and IP address on a name-server) listed.

Making your website user-friendly is vital. Making it accessible to search engines is just as important, because this will drive traffic you can't personally reach. **Search engine optimization (SEO)** is an industry all its own and requires a comprehensive understanding of exactly how the major search engines (Google, Yahoo, Bing) find and categorize your site. The algorithms they use change constantly and unless the formulas are leaked, there's no way of knowing exactly how your site is indexed. This topic is beyond the scope of this book, but I will give you a few key components that ensure your web pages are found by spiders (or bots – the pieces of code that go out and search the internet to bring back information that is indexed by the search engine),

regardless of the exact algorithms. These are:

- **High quality content**. Use appropriate keywords but don't resort to "keyword stuffing". Provide informative, interesting copy that visitors want to read. *Content is king*.

- Upload **various forms of media**: video, audio, graphics, photos, text. Don't forget to add keywords and descriptions to all; search engine spiders can't see or hear (also handy for accommodating visual or hearing impaired human visitors).

- **Update the content** frequently (easier to do with a blog rather than a traditional site). Every time you add something new it provides a fresh opportunity for search engine bots to re-index and rate your site.

- **Build links** between pages and pieces of content on your site as well as between your site and others. This is easily accomplished with a **link exchange**. A **sponsored link** on a high-quality, outside site is also beneficial. Search engine spiders look for the amount of inbound and outbound traffic from your pages to assign a ranking.

- **Between-page links** make your site more easily navigable, too. The easier it is for a human visitor to move around the site, the better search engine bots can do so, as well. Always include an **RSS feed** so visitors and bots alike can see your updates immediately.

- **Encourage communication**. Every comment on your **blog** post with a link to another site increases ranking – in direct correlation to the other site's ranking (so don't use "link farms").

Consider SEO in conjunction with the purpose of your site. A commercial website should perform one of two (or both) functions: actual sales or a sales funnel. Retail businesses are likely to use their website for actual sales. Companies that offer services will benefit more from turning their website into a sales funnel. In this instance, the idea is to drive traffic to your pages so that you entice visitors to **opt-in** (complete a short form with name and email address) and receive future marketing materials. Once someone has agreed to allow you to contact them, you've just increased the size of your database. You've also been given a golden opportunity to establish a relationship that just might turn your opt-in into a buyer. Most businesses can benefit from both website functions.

Getting visitors to opt-in to receive your marketing message can be tricky. Too many people are inundated with spam in their email inbox every day and they are often hesitant to provide their personal contact information. That's why you should offer an enticement – something for free. It could be a special report, a white paper, a top 10 list, a how-to guide, a video clip, an **eBook**, or nearly anything else you can think of. Most of these items don't cost anything other than a bit of your time, but to your website visitor, they represent something of value. Remember the law of reciprocity that drives human behavior; or the old "you scratch my back I'll scratch yours" mentality.

And because you're a busy small business owner, you need to automate the freebie and the subsequent messages you send to your online database. There are lots of software programs available to perform this function – everything from the free version of Constant Contact to the ultra-powerful, feature-packed Infusionsoft. With an **auto responder** system in place, visitors opt-in and receive their freebie within seconds. It also allows you to send a mass message to everyone in your database in the future (fulfilling the concept of repetition and consistency).

Interactive Advertising and Brilliant Automation

When it comes to advertising the Mad Men of the 1960s could only dream about, Evolution Bureau (EVB) has cornered the market. This company is the brains behind such brilliant interactive marketing as Office Max's Elf Yourself, Kodak's Make Me Super, and Orbit Gum's Fabulous Orbit Name Revealer on Facebook.

EVB saw the revolution coming when social media first became popular. They quickly identified that the best way to engage consumers in a relationship that might never be face-to-face was to entertain them. An app, a game, or a fun activity are ways to make advertising seem like something else, engage and entertain, and spread content virally across the World Wide Web with little encouragement.

People participation is the key to going viral through interactivity. One of EVB's more recent campaigns was a promotion for the season premiere episode of Criss Angel's *Mindfreak* on the A&E network.

Criss, of course, is known for his over-the-top illusions and magic tricks. So EVB took that concept and brought it online with an interactive campaign the likes of which has never before been seen. The campaign was entitled Freak Your Mind. They set up a simple landing page that allowed visitors to input the name, email address, and phone number of their friends. Immediately afterward, an email was generated and sent to the friend with the link to a URL and a message asking them to watch a video of Criss. When the recipient clicked on the site, they were shocked to view Criss doing a card trick where the magician would reveal a card showing the person's name and phone number. This was followed by an automatic voice or text message urging the person to view the show.

The term blog is a shortened version of weblog. In 1999, there were a total of 23 blogs listed. Not until Pitas introduced a DIY blog platform later that year did the number reach the hundreds. Today they are too numerous to count.

The end result? Nearly three million visitors used the interactive site and the season premiere of *Criss Angel: Mindfreak* became the highest-rated cable show in its time slot as well as the highest rated episode in the show's history.

When you create your website, why not add a **blog**? Then again, you can use a blogging platform such as WordPress to build your entire site. This platform contains such diverse functionality and wide variety of widgets that it can be impossible to tell the difference between a traditional site and one developed with WordPress. This is a great way to keep your online content fresh and invite interaction via comments. Yes, it takes time to write blog posts and upload/update content. Although you can schedule posts well in advance, someone still has to do the writing. But the key to effective blogging is to offer a source of valuable information which, in turn, establishes you as an authority on a subject integral to your industry. More than just informative, a good blog post can be humorous, interesting, entertaining, or thought-provoking. Any of these are good marketing tools because they pique visitors' curiosity and keep them returning to your site for more. They also encourage communication via commenting.

Here's a trick to making your blog posts work overtime. As soon as you post a new one, submit the URL and a brief description with appropriate keywords to **social bookmarking** sites such as Del.icio.us, Digg, Reddit, Furl, or StumbleUpon. This greatly increases the post's exposure as well as building an inbound link to your page. You will have to set up an account at each social bookmarking site but once you've done that, it's simple to write a description and copy and paste for each submission. The five sites I've listed here are currently some of the most popular, but if you want more exposure, you can certainly use others as well.

What other elements should your website include in addition to a blog? Outside of the obvious contact information, company description and logo, and product or service information, there are a host of other items you can upload that make a visitor's experience more entertaining and interactive. Include a downloadable

eBrochure, a **video** clip (footage from a conference, a talking business card, etc.), an audio **podcast** (an interview or perhaps a reading from a chapter of your eBook), and a **forum** for members. Encourage interaction and entice visitors to return by hosting an **online contest** or starting an opinion **survey** – instruct participants to return on a specific day to view the results. The more you can make your website about *the visitor*, and not about you, the greater your chances of driving traffic and establishing relationships.

Or how about something fun and a bit different? You could add an application that allows visitors to create an **eGreeting card** they can email to their friends; make sure it contains your company logo or meme. You can also provide an **online game** to play, something that teaches the player about a topic related to your business or a competitive strategy game that moves through the various rooms in your building or office. A multi-player game is your best bet to promote a bit of healthy competition and keep people coming back to your site on a regular basis.

If you want your game to go viral, try creating an online app such as "Elf Yourself" or "Yearbook Yourself". Both of these have been wildly popular in recent years. They allow you to use a photo of your face (or someone else's) and superimpose it on an animated cartoon character (a dancing elf) or beneath the most popular hairstyles of decades past (gleaned from old yearbooks). Windows Live Messenger lets you create an icon with the hairstyle, lips, and accessories of your choice while AMC.com has a special Mad Men page where you can develop your own character based on those in the TV series. The possibilities are nearly endless and the net result is an online application likely to go viral just because it's *fun*.

Finally, if your website sells products with an online shopping cart, don't miss the opportunity to **upsell** by suggesting related items or services. Online retail giant Amazon does this particularly well with its automatically propagated list headlined "Customers who bought X also purchased...." If you sell high dollar items, you could also suggest the customer purchase an extended warranty or service plan.

Once you've got your website and blog up and running, take a dive into **social media** – one of the fastest ways to spread your message and encourage personal connections.

Social Media

Web 2.0 marketing is all about using **social media** sites like Facebook, Twitter, YouTube, and LinkedIn (the top four social media sites for businesses) to establish a relationship with your target market. It all begins with an account optimized to show off your business and a commitment to frequent contributions.

Start by setting up your accounts. You will want to include as much personalization and informational content as possible. This includes your company logo, pictures, video, website links, and your business objective.

For Twitter, you must keep the account description to 86 characters but you can add a nice background image that says more. Keywords are very important in that they allow other users to find you based on your industry and specialties.

Facebook allows you to add video content and a welcome tab to your page, both of which are great adjuncts to the general information about your company. But, because Facebook is largely a personal connection site, you also need to include the information that makes you human, not just a company.

LinkedIn is a wonderful B2B tool for using your connections to find prospective clients and it has a host of apps that connect to your blog and other social media accounts. The important information to include on your LinkedIn profile is your industry experience, memberships, and education. The more thorough you make these sections, the more likely it is that someone will find you based on your professional connections.

YouTube's tag line is "Broadcast yourself" and it allows you to do just that, with a profile, personal connections, and an app that links to your Facebook account. Post as many videos as you can, which will increase your ranking and entice more followers. YouTube is all about entertainment value so dry, boring video content isn't going to attract anyone, but humorous or interesting videos will. Repurpose the video content on your website by uploading it to YouTube in order to get the most bang for your buck.

For any social media site, take the time to fill out all the boxes and tabs and upload as much content in as many forms as you can. Again, this takes time but it is well worth the effort. A fully optimized, professional social media account denotes a professional company.

Not only do you need to create your customized account, but you need to post often, contact others, and start conversations. The goal is to reach out to prospects and develop an online relationship. You can't accomplish this if you aren't an active user. Luckily there are free online tools, such as Social Oomph, which allow you to write tweets and schedule them in advance. For a nominal monthly fee, this online software allows you to do the same for your Facebook account.

The latest news in the world of marketing is a big change to Twitter. A common complaint is that photos and video can only be posted to the site via a website link – they can't be instantly viewed. Twitter is now changing that by providing a split screen; when someone clicks on a link in a tweet, an additional screen pops up showing the content right alongside the list of tweets. This makes Twitter an even more vital component of social media marketing.

Perhaps the biggest mistake small business owners make in the social media arena is not understanding its real purpose. Sure, it would be great if you sold something as a direct result of posting a link to your website, but the truth is that this rarely happens. So instead of making continuous, hard sales pitches, consider social media a virtual cocktail party. Discuss current happenings. Tell a story. Share news. Ask questions. Join ongoing discussions or start one yourself. Respond to others. Retweet someone else's posts. Just like your website, make it more about the prospective client and not yourself. Social media success is based on give and take, talking and listening, sharing and providing.

Five of the best ways you can use social sites to further your business relationships:

1. Develop a **group of fans** interested in your offerings – use a commonality and name your "tribe" to make them feel like an exclusive community.

2. **Offer valuable information and advice** for free; think of this as an ethical bribe that works on the law of reciprocity.

3. **Listen** to what others have to say about your company (use Social Oomph to track references whenever your business name is used with the hash tag or @ symbol).

4. **Track** what your competitors are doing and saying.

5. **Reach out** to current customers with personal contact while looking for new ones.

Don't make it difficult for people to find your business online through social media. Use icons and account links on your website and blog, in your email signature, and on all your printed materials.

One last way to use social media to your advantage is to create a **social group** on LinkedIn and Facebook. This is very straightforward on LinkedIn; with Facebook you have the option to create a group, an official page, or a community page, depending on your business structure and purpose. Official pages used to be referred to as "fan pages". Whichever format you choose, be sure to offer comprehensive information as well as getting, and keeping, discussions going amongst members. And don't forget to check in with your group often to answer questions and respond to comments. It's this type of human interaction that wins over a customer.

The explosion of social media paved the way for another form of marketing that is perfectly suited to the World Wide Web. **Viral** or **referral marketing** can be found all over the internet, but particularly on social networking sites. Because of their popularity, more and more consumers are exclusively using the advice of online friends and family to make a purchase offline. Numerous studies have shown the value of viral marketing over other forms of advertising. After all, wouldn't you trust the opinion of a close friend over a stranger, or even the company itself?

Viral marketing refers to any commercial message that is spread via online users to others. One of the earliest examples of a brilliant viral marketing campaign is Hotmail. From its inception, anyone who signed up for a free email account with MSN had a small line added to the bottom of their messages: "Get your private, free email at http://www.hotmail.com". The more people who created an account, the further this short little message spread.

Quite possibly the first video to ever go viral was entitled "Numa Numa". It's a young Romanian gentlemen yodeling.

AOL did the same thing back in the 1980s by mailing a CD preloaded with software to saturate the market. Who in the 80s didn't have an AOL email account or use AOL to surf the 'net? For at least a decade, the company literally ruled the World Wide Web because they made it easy to sign up and kept their direct mail campaign going for years.

I Want My Maypo, My MTV, and My Tommy Hilfiger

When it comes to viral marketing, George Lois is the original. An icon of the adverting industry for over six decades, Lois seemed to instinctively know what to do to make a person, company, or brand famous overnight.

His viral marketing campaigns began with Maypo, a cereal that was most often associated with baby food. How to grab a bigger marketing share by introducing it as an adult breakfast food? Lois took some of the biggest sports figures of the time, including Mickey Mantle, Don Meredith, and Johnny Unitas and turned them into big sissies. Each spot featured an athlete whining, "I want my Maypo!"

Lois would take that same concept and use it some 25 years later, in 1982. At that time, MTV was brand new and struggling to become syndicated on national television stations. A series of TV spots featuring VJs – and even Mick Jagger! – all saying "I want my MTV" along with a message to the viewer to call their cable company and ask that the station be offered in their viewing area, worked brilliantly. In a matter of hours, MTV was airing across the nation and quickly became the station of choice for millions of teens, college students, and young adults.

Fast forward a few years to a young designer who enlisted George Lois' agency to help him develop a name in the fashion industry. This unknown fashion designer had been told by other Madison Avenue agencies that it would take millions of dollars and many years before his brand could be established.

Lois knew that was rubbish. He started by creating a billboard ad. The copy read: "The 4 Great American Designers for Men are…R___L___, P___E___, C___K___, and T___H___." A logo of the unknown fourth designer was placed below the fill-in-the-blanks text. There was an instant buzz in Manhattan. Who in the world was TH and why did he think he should be considered a great designer? People went crazy trying to figure out the answer by matching the logo to the designer.

Overnight, Tommy Hilfiger was the newest name in must-have fashions for the family. A week later, he was the featured guest on The

Johnny Carson Show. According to Hilfiger, Lois' brilliant campaign, "turbo charged" his success, causing him to work night and day to make enough product available for the heightened demand.

Viral marketing is not limited to the internet. It can occur anywhere, at any time, via any media. And George Lois is proof of that.

Both of these campaigns worked incredibly well. This is due to the key components of any successful viral marketing campaign:

1) Give away something for free

2) Make it easy to share

3) Make the campaign scalable (you don't want to run out of whatever you're offering if demand is larger than expected)

4) Exploit human motivations (greed, popularity, kinship)

5) Use existing social networks to reach the circle of influence

6) Spread the message vertically as well as horizontally (to other websites in addition to people)

You can do the same thing that Hotmail did. Your freebie might be a special report, a video clip, or an iPhone app. Post it on your website or blog and add a row of social bookmarking buttons (provided by sites such as AddThis.com or SocializeThis.com) to make it easy to share. Send an email message to your full database and include a simple, clickable link to share the URL with friends. Post the link to the freebie via your social media updates and social bookmarking accounts. Partner with non-competing websites that will agree to add a small blurb and link on their pages. Once it catches on, your message will spread like wildfire, increasing brand awareness and driving traffic to your site.

If your budget allows, consider running a **Facebook ad**. Facebook offers two payment options: cost per click (CPC) or cost per thousand impressions (CPM), which allows you to stay within your Main Street budget.

The advantages of banner advertising on this social media site are the insane popularity of the site and the great degree of customization available. If you only want members who enjoy specific hobbies, fit into a specified age range, or are located in a particular area to see your ad, you can put these restrictions in place regarding your ad placement. This is another type of target audience advertising since it works with the hobbies and interests already specified by the sites' members. And as the most popular social networking site on the internet, Facebook ads really extend your market reach in a very targeted, effective manner.

> *Research firm eMarketer expects social media advertising spending to reach $1.7 billion in 2010, half of that for Facebook ads alone.*

Pay Per Click Advertising Campaigns

Banner advertising isn't limited to Facebook. A **pay per click (PPC) campaign** on any of the major search engines (Google,

Yahoo, and Bing) is also a very effective form of online advertising – although this is one of the more costly forms. You bid on the price you will pay per click for designated keywords.

One way to make it more affordable is to stay away from bidding on the most popular keywords. The more popular a search term is, the more you need to bid for top placement.

Although recessionary ad spending has been down overall in the past two years, online advertising, particularly with video content, is the only segment continuing to grow. Search marketing spending numbers are down, but only because the cost has decreased. The biggest companies spend a huge percentage of their budget to ensure they come up first in search engine results for the most popular keywords.

Consider using long-tail keywords instead. The long tail refers to the end of a bell graph – the diminishing line on the right that tapers down to zero. The most commonly used keywords comprise the big bell at the apex of the graph. Those search terms that are still relevant but used less frequently are included in the long tail. Obviously you don't want to bid on keywords that are not descriptive of your business, but there is an advantage to using long-tail phrases since they reach more targeted prospects (the search term "high quality widgets in Timbuktu" is used by a serious prospect where the keyword phrase "cheap widgets" is not). In addition, this type of campaign is based on less competition and results in a cheaper click rate. Pick out the long-tail keywords that best describe your particular business niche and they could actually net you a larger profit.

A new format for PPC advertising is **option ads**. Pioneered by Hulu, this lets the viewer choose which type of advertisements they wish to view while watching a program. An example is three different ads for a brand offering hair care products. The consumer's choice is whether they'd like to view spots featuring products for fine, thick, or frizzy hair. As an advertiser, you can ensure viewers watch your ads, but the advantage of option advertising is showing them the particular type of product or service they are most likely to purchase based on preference or need.

As Web 2.0 PPC ads continue to develop, the next wave is **real-time online advertising**. All the major search engines are now offering real-time bidding that brings up your ad in the fractions of a second between the time someone types in the URL of a particular site and the page appears. Bidding is based on the content of the page being directly accessed, the profile of the user, and price. So, while a person is waiting for ESPN's home page to load, a company offering sports equipment can specify that their ad be brought up instantly. The same thing can happen for a competitor's site, allowing a competing company to get their foot in the door, virtually speaking (e.g. a visitor searching for the Barnes & Noble site sees a banner ad for Fictionwise).

And finally, yet another form of PPC advertising is **interactive ads**. These are dynamic banners that change with a simple click or mouse-over meant to engage the user rather than appear as an overt advertisement. The Webby Awards even have a category exclusively for each year's best interactive ads. A recent winner was Pringle's. Their banner ad showed a woman with one hand inside a Pringle's chip can and a man kneeling before her with an opened engagement ring box. Each click of a little cartoon man icon with a moustache in the corner changes the heading to about a hundred different sayings, starting with a funny caption and moving on to a "dialogue" with the Pringle's man. This type of advertising looks less like a commercial and more like a game. Why does it work? Because it's *fun* – and funny.

Don't discount the power of humor. Goodby & Silverstein created the Budweiser commercial initially run during the 1998 Super Bowl using lizards brought on board to replace the famous frogs, Bud, Weis, and Er. The campaign was actually titled "Kill the Frogs". In this particular ad, one of the all-time favorites in Super Bowl advertising history, two lizards with Brooklyn accents hire a hit man ferret to do the frogs in via electrocution by flashing neon Budweiser sign. The frogs survived, as did the one of the best punch lines of humorous commercials, "Eventually every frog has to croak." Did it sell a lot of beer? Maybe. But what worked was the fact that the ad was just funny, and that made it memorable. The same concept can be applied to any online interactive ad campaign. When it comes to unforgettable content most likely to go viral, funny trumps serious every time.

For any PPC ad campaign follow these best practices for the greatest success:

- Develop a **customized landing page** for your ad. This page should be highly relevant to the search terms you are bidding on and not more than one click away from the call to action.

- **Split test**: experiment with various offers, designs, and text to see which ad design results in the highest amount of click-throughs.

- **Track** the campaign frequently; change the ad quickly if click-throughs aren't resulting in sales.

- **Geotargeting**: If your business is local or regional, consider limiting your ads based on the user's location.

More Online Advertising Opportunities

Do you enjoy writing? If so, there are many ways you can advertise your business online for free. Remember that the more places you have content that links to your website, the greater SEO benefit.

Do a search for blogs on topics related to your industry or niche and offer to write a **guest blog post**. For instance, if your company sells tools for auto repair, partner with a blog that provides instructions for vehicle maintenance tasks. Ask the owner of the blog to schedule it in advance so you can hype it up; take time on the scheduled day of your post to read through comments and respond, making a connection with new prospects.

Write an **e-zine**. This is just like a digital newsletter you can post online and/or email to your database. Provide informative articles, news about your business, testimonials, and some fun things like a contest or interesting trivia. Photos of your staff and offices are good, too. You may also want to include a special offer available only to readers of the e-zine; encourage your existing database to forward each issue to their contacts. E-zines are most effective if you write and distribute them on a regular basis, perhaps once a month or so. They can also be monetized; when you build up subscribership of your e-zine, you can charge a small fee for including ads from other companies.

Write articles and submit them to online **article directories**, such as EzineArticles.com. Directories do a lot of marketing and backend SEO to make content on their sites appear at the top of search results. Your marketing opportunity comes from the brief author bio included with each article submitted; always add your website address so readers can easily access more information. If you can write and submit lots of articles, this is a great way to become known as an authority in your industry.

Tip: *repurpose a blog post by turning it into an article, or vice versa. Do change it enough so that it is not seen as duplicate content, however – a big no-no with search engines.*

Post to **online bulletin/message boards**. Where once bulletin boards were a very popular way of interacting on the internet, they are now more often in the form of online forums and message boards (sites like Freecycle for exchanging goods or Gaia.com for gaming enthusiasts). As long as the topic of the message board is related in some way to your business, the time you spend there posting and answering questions allows you to create relationships that could translate to referrals or sales.

Add your company to **online business directories**. This is particularly useful if yours has a regional customer base. Business directories on the web are akin to printed telephone books; they usually include your logo, contact information, map of your location, link to your website, and reviews from past patrons. There are numerous directories available – everything from the big search engine directories on Yahoo and Google to small, local aggregation sites. There is usually a fee associated with an upgraded account that may allow you to post photos and your company logo, so do a comparison between the sites available and see what fits best into your marketing plan.

David T. Fagan & Aaron Halderman

Old school seminars usually involved gathering a group in a physical location and making your presentation to attendees face-to-face. Today, **webinars** are quickly taking their place. Rather than having to worry about travel costs and meeting space rental, online webinars use software, such as WebEx or GoToMeeting, that allows multiple users to log into a site all at the same time and view the presentation in real time. The site is visually interactive, allowing the presenter to share a screen that lets participants follow the action. There is a cost to use the software, either one time or a monthly subscription fee. If your business frequently offers new products, webinars are ideal for demonstration and the cost for an annual subscription to the software usually costs less.

The last internet marketing method we will examine is **iPhone** or **smartphone apps**. This is one of the newest, most modern ways of providing a marketing venue for your company. The idea is to create an application that is useful to your customers and prospects – a unique value not offered by others – and allows them to easily connect to your online offerings. You could also develop an application for sale, bringing incremental revenue to your bottom line.

Making your own smartphone app can be tricky; it takes some bit of technical expertise and if you are marketing an app for the iPhone, you must get Apple's approval before it is offered. Still, if you have a techie guru in your office, this could be an excellent way to reach a target market of rapidly growing smart phone users. It just might be a great way to stand out from your competition, as well.

To keep up on marketing in the world of Web 2.0, you can't be afraid of technology. The savvy small business owner will do his or her best to keep up on the latest innovations, such as the iPad and new mobile devices, to stay one – or two or three or four – steps ahead of the competition. Smaller screen size and limited accessibility via handheld devices requires changes to your online content. Communication techniques are changing rapidly and it's up to you to change along with it if your goal is to grow your company's profitability.

I'll wrap up this chapter with a quote from author Mary J. Cronin, "For many businesses, the internet is still a technology in search of a strategy." Use the strategy outlined in your marketing plan and always keep your goals in sight. Technology needn't be frightening, especially when you stick to your marketing road map and view the internet as your friend instead of foe.

Chapter Five: Signage – Getting People to Take a Second Look

"You can see a lot just by looking." – Yogi Berra

There are many ways to use signage for advertising. Take a look at this list of the top 16 mad ad signs for small business owners:

1. Graphic Wraps
2. Digital Menu Boards
3. Shopping cart ads
4. Public Restrooms
5. Bulletin Boards
6. Billboards
7. Banners
8. Spinners
9. Sandwich Boards
10. Park Bench
11. Bus
12. Cabs
13. Mobile billboards (trucks)
14. Vehicle Magnets or Wraps
15. Yard Signs
16. Hot air balloons, blimps, planes

Signage is one of the oldest forms of advertising. If you think about it, even the cavemen used signs by scratching pictographs onto the walls of their caves. It is postulated that these symbols and pictures sent a message to others who came upon the cave later. When we became more civilized, merchants often painted scenes on the outside of buildings while street vendors held up a small placard with a picture to indicate the type of merchandise they peddled. By the late fourteenth century, taverns in Europe were identified by handsome painted signs over the door to the establishment. From there, signage used for advertising really caught on. The addition of neon tubes and electric illumination ensured that patrons could find a business at night – and kept the advertising message glowing even after dark.

Burma Shave was one of the most innovative companies of the mid-20th century. They used a series of 6 small roadside signs to form a memorable jingle such as:
Our fortune/
Is your/
Shaven face/
It's our best/
Advertising space/
Burma Shave

Of course now we see signs everywhere. Remember that old song from the 1960s with the refrain of "Sign, sign, everywhere a sign"? It is difficult for the small business marketer to stand out amongst the big billboards and flashy design of franchises and

95

large corporations. Difficult – but not impossible. All it takes is some creativity and a focus zeroed in on your target market. Keep the message visual and the text short; rarely does a potential customer have the time to sit and peruse lengthy copy but a catchy graphic will stick in the mind (Burma Shave's forte). Signs are only effective if they reach prospects where they go – and then are appealing enough to catch someone's eye.

That is the most important take away from this chapter and deserves repeating: *advertising signs must be placed where they will be noticed by your target market.* Are teenagers likely to buy the family's groceries at the supermarket? Is the person having financial problems apt to use a taxi for transportation? Most likely not. Sure, they might, but remember what I advised in Chapter Three: it's better to design your advertising around the one person who is a likely prospect than the 99 others who probably aren't interested in your offerings.

Creating your signs can be accomplished with any desktop publishing software program and a computer printer. If you need a bigger size than the standard 8 x 10, send the file to your local printer who has a machine that handles larger paper. Professional printing is often more affordable than you at first think. Online sites such as VistaPrint offer lots of loss leader freebies and very reasonably priced oversized postcards, tri-fold brochures (which you can cut into thirds), business cards, posters, and magnets.

I've categorized advertising signage as indoor and outdoor. Because people really can't get anywhere without traveling first, I encourage you to use both. And one of the best things about the types of signs discussed here is they are inexpensive, allowing for a lot of exposure for a small cost.

Indoor Signage

Any place where the public gathers presents an opportunity for your advertising. Think of all the buildings where thousands or even millions of consumers pass through each and every day: train stations, airports, parking garages, retail stores, concert halls, museums, libraries, churches, fraternal clubhouses, schools, community rec centers, bars, restaurants...the list goes on and on. You might immediately think about eliminating some of the sites in this list because you've never seen advertising there. But don't be so quick to judge. Just because it's never been done before doesn't mean it is impossible. I'll just bet if you donated money, time, or products to an organization you would be compensated with at least a small interior sign in exchange for your contribution.

Transportation hubs present the best opportunity to reaching the greatest number of consumers. Anyone who commutes to work or travels on a regular basis has to use either a plane, train, subway, light rail, bus, or parking garage. The only problem is catching the eye of busy travelers. You must really be creative to make people pay attention to your advertisements. A shocking image, beautiful artwork, or a simple question against a clean backdrop are just some of the ways companies have advertised effectively and stand out amidst the hustle and bustle of a busy station.

Graphic wraps are a new way to put your creativity to good use. The sky is the limit when it comes to devising a quirky, unique way to place your message where it will be noticed. Some of the more creative examples of graphic wraps are:

- A staircase made to look like suitcases with a travel agency website address painted at the bottom of the flight;

- Parking garage supports wrapped to look like giant tees on a golf green with the name of the course printed vertically along the tee shaft;

- An elevator with the picture of a smiling bride and groom – when the doors open the passenger is greeted by a sign against the interior back wall advertising a divorce attorney's services.

These graphic wraps are so unique that not only do they make people do a double take, the message is spread virally due to the "Wow!" factor.

Another fairly new media for your advertising message is a **digital menu board**. These are the continually revolving messages on an LCD screen you might see at a conference center, airport, hotel, or even the Department of Motor Vehicles. Because you have a simple line of text and share exposure with other advertisers, this marketing method is actually quite inexpensive. As long as the venue is correlated with your company's products or services, digital menu boards are bound to be effective; for instance, a restaurant in the neighborhood of a convention center could promote the daily special by posting it on the board conference attendees consult to find their breakout session.

The supermarket is an excellent place to advertise. Who doesn't need to buy groceries? Young or old, single or married, families or couples – everyone eats and drinks and gets their prescriptions filled. I've seen advertisements on both sides of the end of a **shopping cart**, on the pull-down flap near the handle, and on the motorized scooters available for patrons who have difficulty walking. Write short copy that makes the grocery store customer think; something that makes them take action either in the store (best for purveyors of food and beverages) or immediately upon leaving.

Any place that has a bulletin board is perfect to tack up your business card as an impromptu sign. Think of grocery stores, senior centers, RV parks, community centers, chambers of commerce, etc. Always keep a stack of business cards and a small box of thumb tacks handy.

Restrooms in a restaurant, bar, or event center are another good venue for your advertising. When are people most likely to use a public restroom? Wherever they are eating and drinking. And let's face it; when you're in a stall doing your business you've really got nothing else to do but read what's right in front of you. In other words, you've got a captive audience! The patrons tend to be a broad demographic but then again, anyone who can afford to eat and drink out or attend a sporting event is likely to have a good disposable income; so distasteful as it may seem at first, high-end products and services tend to benefit greatly from **restroom signs**. And if you can snag a space on a framed board with printed blocks of ads, this mad ad is quite cheap.

Now that we've covered indoor signage, let's move to the great outdoors.

Outdoor Signage

The options for outdoor signage are nearly limitless. The only limits truly are legal ones; most cities make it illegal to post signs on telephone poles, traffic structures, and public buildings. Outside of this, consider every possibility from the sky to the ground.

Usually meant to attract drivers, outdoor signs need to be very succinct (a handful of words at most) in order to be assimilated within the seconds it takes to pass it. Short, simple messages with a website address or toll-free phone number in a very large, sans-serif font work best. Outdoor signs are best used as an announcement for a new business or as a reminder rather than the sole means of marketing. Their purpose is to strengthen branding and identity, and maybe trigger a buying impulse that makes the driver turn the car around.

Got Bad English?

Advertising agency Goodby & Silverstein were given the American Dairy Association account after their campaign, "Milk: It Does a Body Good" had run its course with little effect on the number of cartons sold. Sure, the tag line was a good one and the spots featured popular athletes of the 1980s. But they were targeted at kids, and kids don't really pay attention unless the commercial is for something new, different, and sweet. Milk is a commodity, not a brand. It can't be made any differently and it had to be advertised generically. As a result, by the end of the "Does a Body Good" campaign, milk sales were actually dropping 4% per year.

During a brainstorming session to come up with an appropriate new tag line, one of the ad execs mentioned, "Do you have milk?" It was a start, but it wasn't catchy enough. From there, the phrase got boiled down to its very core, "Got milk?"

The first response to this tag line was, "It's bad English." This was followed by, "It will never work."

Goodby & Silverstein created a series of ads anyway. They used everything from a group of cats to a picture of an Oreo cookie, a graham cracker, and a brownie. But perhaps the best spot was a TV commercial that showed a man biting into a thick peanut butter sandwich. He's listening to the radio, which airs a trivia contest. The first caller to correctly answer the question wins a prize. The man with the sandwich quickly dials the station and attempts to give his answer. The only problem is he can't be understood due to the peanut butter in his mouth.

He spies a milk container on his desk and frantically pours it into an empty glass only to find mere drops left in the carton. The radio station hangs up on him, unable to understand his correct answer.

Thus begun one of the most effective advertising campaigns of all time. It was splashed across billboards, magazine pages, and supermarket dangler signs. Not only did "Got milk?" increase sales, it was imitated by scores of other companies – and still is today. Remember the last presidential election when one enterprising entrepreneur printed up T-shirts that read "Got Obama?"

Got advertising?

Perhaps the most common form of outdoor signage is a **billboard**. Bright colors, a few well-thought-out power words and a phone number (these days many drivers use Bluetooth with their cell phone, allowing them to call you immediately from their vehicle) is sufficient for your advertising message. Divide the billboard in two and share the space with an advertising partner to keep costs down.

Here's an innovative campaign that used billboard advertising around Los Angeles. The sign simply read "Still a Virgin?" along with a toll-free number to the "Virgin Help Line". What happened when someone called the number? They were treated to a number of options ranging from "Press 1 if you're a virgin" to "Press 4 if you want your virginity back" to "Press 7 if you like to party". Obviously this was just a publicity stunt; in fact the billboards were erected to promote a Will Farrell movie called The Virginity Hit. Parents in the greater L.A. area were horrified that it opened up conversations with their kids they weren't ready to discuss, but the ad had its intended effect. Tens of thousands of people called the number and the buzz around the controversial billboards spread across the country within a matter of days – and that's exactly what was supposed to happen.

For an entrepreneur an equally catchy headline (but perhaps not so controversial) could result in a huge impact to the bottom line. It's the formula of simple, but startling, copy along with a toll-free phone number that works.

Banners, because they can be used for a variety of purposes and places, are a thrifty buy for the small business owner. They can be hung outside your building, taken to craft fairs, festivals, conferences, and seminars, or placed at other businesses (with permission). The key to keeping printed banners affordable is to make the copy timeless. Include the basic information for your company. If you want to use the banner to advertise a special, it's much cheaper to paste a bright yellow vinyl star in one corner with "Clearance Sale Today" on it than it is to print a special banner just for this purpose.

Spinners are much like smaller, sturdier banners. You may have seen people hired to stand outside a business or on a street corner with an arrow-shaped sign, printed on both sides, that a dexterous person can spin around their body. In fact, if you hire the right person to present your spinner, this form of advertising becomes performance art – and that's a good thing. Remember that half the battle of getting your advertising message across is enticing people to pay attention to it. And hey, if you've got kids out of school in the summer who are bored, why not pay them a small amount to stand outside and show their stuff with a spinner sign?

If you want an even cheaper form of advertising, how about a **sandwich board**? Simply constructed from two pieces of lightweight wood and a pair of "suspenders" (for humans) or top support board, these signs are something you could easily create yourself. If you or someone you know is blessed with artistic ability, you can paint a message and simple graphic on each side for little more than the cost of paint and stencils. Few businesses use these signs anymore so they tend to stand out. If you were stopped at a stoplight and saw someone walking around with a pair of boards strapped to their body, wouldn't you take notice? Sandwich boards can also be made stationary and placed in the front of a store. Just like other forms of advertising aimed at drivers, though, make the message simple and clear.

Signs across the back of **park benches** are another way to advertise outdoors. Outside of city parks and bus stops, consider approaching businesses in buildings with a courtyard or landscaped walkways; these are likely to have benches throughout and you can easily target the staff that populates the building with your marketing message.

Metal signs are best for park benches since they will be subjected to sun, wind, and various weather conditions. Traditionally, newspapers and magazines have advertised on benches but there's no reason that you couldn't use this media for showcasing restaurants, snack foods, beverages, books, or anything else people tend to think about while sitting in a park. Park benches are a great opportunity for seasonal advertising, too. Imagine the impact of a CPA reminding the sitter that it's almost tax time or a florist mentioning Mother's Day is coming soon.

And while someone is sitting on a park bench plastered with your advertisement, they just might be waiting to catch a bus emblazoned with another of your signs in the form of a wrap. Now you may be thinking to yourself that a **bus wrap** is an expensive form of advertising. Actually, window, rear end, and interior bus signs are quite reasonable. And if you think outside the box, it can be even more so. Why not ask your local senior citizens center, retirement community, special needs school, or hotel if they are willing to sell ad space on their buses or vans? If your company offers estate planning services, for instance, placing a sign on the outside or interior of the community senior citizens center bus might just bring in new business.

Taxi cabs usually take advertising, too. You may be able to sponsor the topper, or run an ad on an interior LCD screen or printed poster. Just think of all the fares a cab in a big city picks up throughout a single day. This is a great venue to reach business travelers; they are a captive audience for the minutes or hours riding to their destination. For companies selling higher-end products, place your advertising inside a limousine offering airport service. Some taxi services also allow advertisements printed on the back side of receipts. This is an exceptional opportunity since most business travelers keep their receipts in order to get reimbursed.

Two more automotive options are **mobile billboards** and personal **vehicle wraps** or **magnets**. The former is great for reaching drivers stuck in freeway traffic while the latter is highly effective in parking lots. Personally, I've noticed cars parked next to mine at the hardware store and jotted down the phone number or website address listed on the side if it was a business I was interested in. This is a great way to keep your advertising working for you no matter where you venture – and since it's a one-time cost, it's very affordable.

The last type of outdoor signage I recommend is **yard signs**. You know those little squares of plastic attached to a stake most often used by political candidates? There's absolutely no reason you can't utilize them for your business, too. Ask your friends and family members, or neighbors close to your office if they will plant a sign in their front yard. This is a very effective way for businesses such as landscapers, mobile container suppliers, car washes and such to reach prospective clients where they are likely to be thinking of such services. Don't limit yard signs to an actual yard, either. How about a farm or a field? If you supply manure or insecticide to the farmer, a sign that says "Crops courtesy of ABC Agricultural Supply" is a pretty powerful testimonial.

The advertising agency that came up with the idea for sidewalk stickers was being very creative — but it didn't turn out so well in the end. They failed to test the decals beforehand and city crews in San Francisco had to steam them off the pavement. The agency was sued by the city for the cost of cleanup. This is why you need to test, test, test!

When it comes to outdoor advertising, your creative efforts need not be constrained. Recently, an online gaming company used decals on the sidewalks of San Francisco to advertise a new version of their game and it really got a big buzz going – so much that players of the beta version numbered in the millions the first day it was released.

You can also look to the sky. If your budget has room, you can use **hot air balloons**, **blimps**, and **planes** to trail banners or skywrite your message across the wild blue yonder. While this form of advertising can be expensive, you can make it cheaper in conjunction with a scheduled event. Become a sponsor of a local air show and use the opportunity to take your message to the sky – not only can you negotiate free skywriting or a flying banner as part of your sponsorship package, your message will be in the place it is most likely to get noticed by event attendees and neighboring residents alike!

Some businesses have used an old car suspended in the air to advertise (for an auto repair shop or dealership); others place something unusual on the roof like a big plaster horse (good for a feed store) or cow (great option for a steakhouse). Consider chain link fences, auto license plate holders, corn mazes, manhole covers – anything bound to be seen by prospective customers is fair game!

When it comes to signage there are few, if any, places or ways that limit the spread of your marketing message.

Chapter Six: What's in a Name? Branding and Promotion

"Advertising is salesmanship mass produced. No one would bother to use advertising if he could talk to all his prospects face-to-face. But he can't." – Morris Hite

The lowest cost forms of mad ads with the purpose of branding and promotion:

1. Business Cards
2. Coupons
3. Screens
4. Promotional Items/Advertising Specialty
5. Shirts, hats, clothing
6. Free samples
7. Bundling/ Packaging (add to packaged item)
8. Contests
9. Sponsorship
10. Placement ads
11. Special events/ celebrations
12. Voice mail message
13. Local TV appearance
14. Newspaper column
15. Radio show
16. Demonstrations
17. Training courses
18. Free Seminars
19. How To workshops
20. Teleseminars

How do you get consumers to recognize your business with just a simple image or tag line; a logo or a meme? The answer is branding and promotions.

Imagine if McDonald's completely got rid of its golden arches or Coca Cola lost its cursive script (both of which have been tried before, incidentally). You might still recognize their restaurants and products, but they wouldn't send that subconscious message all advertisers hope for: *Buy me now. I'm familiar. You know what to expect when you purchase me.*

The Advertisement Without a Product

Can you actually create brand awareness before product awareness? Apple's Steve Jobs thought so.

The year was 1984. The Apple Macintosh was set to make its first appearance on the consumer market. The year was also the title of a famous sci-fi novel by George Orwell. In it, Orwell depicted a society controlled, manipulated, and micro-managed by an oligarchic government (Big Brother).

Chiat/Day was the advertising agency in charge of the Apple account. They created a very film noir type of commercial set to air during the 1984 Super Bowl. The spot showed rows and rows of blank-stared people dressed in drab uniforms marching through a tunnel while a message from Big Brother airs on a screen before them. All of a sudden a woman in workout shorts and tank top (bearing a cubist-style picture of the Mac computer) comes running through with a big hammer. She is being chased by a unit of security guards. As she nears the screen she hurls the heavy hammer and smashes it. The text at the end of the spot reads, "On January 24th, Apple Computer will introduce Macintosh. And you'll see why 1984 won't be like *1984*."

The director of the piece was Ridley Scott, who had just released the blockbuster movie, *Blade Runner*, the previous year. Scott's directorial services didn't come cheap; the ad cost Apple some $900,000 to create. The company's execs didn't like it and wanted to pull the ad. Steve Jobs was so certain it would be successful, he, along with Chiat/Day, used his own money to run it over the objections of the company's board.

So did the commercial sell Macs even though it never showed the product? You decide. Even today, nearly 30 years later, Apple has forever changed advertising: every professional ad agency uses a Mac due to its superior graphics capabilities. In this instance, the brand came before the product – and it would never be forgotten.

Branding actually does more than breed familiarity; it promotes confidence. When a prospective customer sees your advertising over and over again, they begin to associate your brand with the succinct business objective that is the core of your marketing plan. It's just human nature to select the familiar over the unfamiliar; if you like a particular type of crackers, how likely are you to buy another brand's if they are an unknown? The only way the X brand of crackers can compete is by constantly barraging you with their marketing message and making you aware of their brand's benefits. It takes time to develop confidence and become familiar.

Branding can actually be considered dangerous. Well-known brands produce a Pavlovian response; what little tyke doesn't see McDonald's golden arches and ask mom or dad to stop for a

Unfortunately, the Crocker Bank ad was so successful that the bank didn't have enough collateral to meet demand. They killed the ad shortly after its introduction.

Happy Meal? Be careful what image you associate with your brand; it can be considered a positive, or a negative.

In fact, branding can influence an entire society or culture. Remember the "Me Generation" of the Mad Men era? Ad exec Mary Wells is credited with coining it, if not creating it, through such memorable campaigns as Coca-Cola teaching the world to sing and Clairol hair color showing women exuberantly stating, "It lets me be me."

Nowadays, many commercials use famous music from the past. But back in 1970, it worked the other way around. Crocker Bank hired an advertising agency to target a demographic they were missing amongst their customer base: young people. Although the bank was known for its exceptional customer service, it was viewed as old-fashioned. Roger Nichols and Paul Williams were contracted to write a song for a TV commercial featuring a young couple getting married and showing how Crocker Bank could help them with their first mortgage and joint bank accounts. The song became a #1 hit that year when "We've Only Just Begun" was recorded by the Carpenters and went on to become one of the most popular tunes played at weddings across the nation.

Change Culture by Just Doing It!

A brand can certainly influence society. One brand that knows how to do this, and do it extremely well is Nike, under the guidance of advertising agency Weiden & Kennedy.

It was during a meeting between the advertising execs and the Nike management team that one of the most famous slogans of all time was created. Reportedly, Dan Weiden complimented the company, saying, "You Nike guys; you just do it." Other sources say the original phrase was "Let's do it." Regardless of its true source, a new campaign that would resonate with people worldwide was born.

The purpose of the campaign, of course, was to increase sales. And it did that admirably, increasing its share of the sports shoe market to a whopping 43% in the years between the end of the 1980s and 1998. But in addition to selling a whole lot of athletic shoes, the Just Do It campaign incited people everywhere – young and old, male and female – to get up and get moving.

Featuring such sports heroes as Bo Jackson and Michael Jordan, the ads themselves rarely showed more than the famous swoosh logo to indicate what product was being offered. Instead, gritty images and sometimes humorous one-liners were meant to show the benefits of being active.

Celebrity endorsements did more than just promote the brand, they made it cool. It represented the hard work and physical exertion associated with being in shape. And even if someone wore a pair of Nikes for fashion more than athletics, it made them look as if they were just as sports-minded as John McEnroe.

Later spinoffs of the Just Do It campaign included a focus on women, with ads portraying a series of young girls exhorting, "Let me play sports."

Nike's Just Do It advertising campaign would forever change American society in a positive manner. And that's just plain good branding – and good marketing.

Promotion works right alongside branding and it is one of the most effective forms of building confidence and breeding familiarity. Promotional materials show your presence in the community, whether it's an online or offline, local or global community. Promotions – particularly as part of public relations – establish your credibility. Don't you think that X brand of crackers could really benefit by promoting their goods through free tastings at the grocery store?

Branding and promotions do not necessarily impact your bottom line in an immediate way, nor are they meant to. I know I said that all advertising needs to be tied to profits. The benefits of familiarity and confidence through branding and promo are sure to increase sales and profitability – over time. This is the part of your marketing plan that relates to commitment and patience. Just as Morris Hite said, you can't meet each prospect face to face and personally relate your passenger story so other advertising materials will have to do so in your stead.

Most of the promotional items in this chapter I recommend that you give away for free. Yes, it's going to cost you to brand and promote your business. But the smart entrepreneur will ask for something in exchange for these freebies; namely opting in to receive future promotional announcements. Hook your prospects with a giveaway, then reel them in over future months with your consistent and regular marketing message.

Now you know the purpose of branding and promotions. Let's take a look at how to brand and promote your business.

Visuals

There are a number of inexpensive items you can use to connect a visual representation of your company with its objective. The majority of people make a more permanent connection when they are presented with a visual aid in addition to reading text or listening to someone speak. And that's the idea behind creating promotional products that work to increase familiarity, confidence, and ultimately profitability.

Let's start with the most basic of all business collateral: **business cards**. It's amazing to me how many entrepreneurs put such little thought into such a potentially powerful marketing piece. I've seen business cards that were little more than a photo, a name, and a phone number. Really? Would you really want to spend money creating something so useless?

How often have you attended networking events where business cards are exchanged only to empty our wallet or purse sometime later because those cards mean nothing? They're just taking up space. Sure, you might hang on to those that represent a good sales lead or prospective joint venture partner. But how many of them get tossed into the trash without a second thought?

If you think of your business card as an advertisement, it will greatly change the way you design it. These days you rarely need more than a phone number and website address along with your name and logo to get the basics across. But that leaves a whole lot of white space – both front and back – that serves no purpose. Why not turn that wasted space into an advertisement for your company? Some of the most creative business cards I've seen use something related to the company's offerings; for instance, a dentist's card with teeth impressions or a thread of dental floss running through the paper, an embroidery company with stitching across one corner, a movie theatre manager's card that resembles a ticket. The back side can become a coupon or punch card (e.g. get one free after 10 purchases), a calendar, a list of trivia, a short quiz, a map of your business location…use your imagination.

While you are handing out business cards, why not include a **coupon**, too? This is especially helpful for start-ups. As you will recall we discussed how branding and promo creates familiarity. A coupon allows a prospective customer to try out your products or services for free. You can bet that if they like your offerings, they'll be back for more and will spread the word to their family, friends, and acquaintances. Use coupons just about anywhere – leave them on the reception counter at a "partner" business, send them via email to your database and encourage the recipients to forward to friends; add them to goody bags at seminars or other events; give a handful to your local Chamber of Commerce; tack several to a bulletin board; place them under the windshield wipers of cars in a parking lot; direct mail them to a new database; slip them through the mail slots in an office building. A little bit of printing can go a lot way.

Do you know the first company to use coupons as a way of increasing sales? None other than Coca-Cola. In 1894, the owner hand wrote slips of paper that could be exchanged for a free glass of soda. Ten years later, Coca-Cola was offered in every state.

A professionally printed pop-up or **display screen** with stand is a useful tool when advertising your business outside the office. Any small business owner who frequently attends trade shows, seminars, conferences and the like as a vendor should always have a screen to erect. Just like a banner, the information on your screen should be timeless, but compelling. The design needs to be something that makes people stop in their tracks and want to find out more about your company. Consider a graphic that looks like a newspaper or magazine cover; a "3D" image that seems to come right off the screen; a zipper that is opening to reveal a product underneath. Definitely include your logo, but if it does not explain exactly what your company is and what it offers, add text that helps people quickly determine if you can supply their needs (what's in it for them).

Tangible Items

There are any number of products you can buy that are customized for your business. These days there is hardly anything you can't use as a **promotional item**. These are also referred to as **advertising specialties**. Some of the most common items are water bottles, flash drives, pens, mouse pads, and the like.

The important thing to remember as you flip through the pages of an advertising specialty catalog is to correlate your promotional item with your specific business and its niche. A dentist might want to invest in small packets of floss with his logo and phone number. A cooking school could give away aprons. A car wash could use air fresheners. You get the idea. This makes for a memorable association between the giveaway and the business itself.

Promotional items are ideal to include as part of a direct mailing to a new database. Of course, they are also almost required at trade shows and conventions, fairs and festivals, networking events and sales calls.

Shirts, hats, and other items of **clothing** work wonderfully for promoting your company in ways you cannot imagine. Remember the example I gave you of Aunt Mabel seeing the company van pull up to her neighbor's house with uniformed employees delivering the goods? This is branding at its best. But even if you give away these items to people outside your organization, they will work to your advantage. Imagine this scenario: your sister is wearing your company's t-shirt while waiting for her car to be serviced; the person across the room sees it and strikes up a conversation, asking questions about the business. Include your URL in the design and she may even feel inclined to visit your website. As long as the design and message are memorable, small things like clothing can make a big impact.

Another method of getting someone to try your business for the first time is to provide **free samples** of your product. A small sample is an ideal direct mail stuffer but might work even better if you set up a booth at a trade show or fair and hand them out personally. How many times have you been at the grocery store, tasted a sample in the store, then added the product to your cart? The "try it then buy it" concept has a long history of converting customers.

Free samples needn't be limited to food. Perhaps you are an author. How about setting up a table at your local library and handing out CDs with the first chapter of your book – or even a complete short story? A nursery could attend a local event and pass out small pots of herbs. Does your company sell pet treats? Ask the local feed or pet supply store to slip one of your packaged treats into each bag of purchases. Giving away a free sample is an excellent way to promote brand awareness and familiarity as well as instill confidence.

When you want to get your product into the hands of many consumers, consider **bundling** or packaging it with another product. The most famous example of this concept is McDonald's Happy Meals. Disney partners with McDonald's to include a toy from their latest movie release in each boxed meal they sell. Kids get the toy, think it's cool, and ask mom if they can go see the movie. In this way, Disney is effortlessly accessing the customers of McDonald's, extending their (already vast) marketing reach.

You can do the same thing on a smaller scale. Talk to the manager at a nearby hotel if you are in the business of providing spa, beauty, or business services. Negotiate a deal to add a coupon or a small item to each of the guest welcome baskets available for purchase. Lots of retailers could easily partner with a company that makes gift baskets or stuffed balloons. Offer your partner a discounted rate on the goods or come up with a plan to share a percentage of sales.

You can also bundle your own products or services and offer the package at a price less than the cost to purchase individual items. This is seen as a real value to consumers and often results in upsales to customers who would have only bought one item as opposed to the more expensive package. Custom bundles are another option; allow the customer to pick and choose from a list and create their own package.

Here's a good form of advertisement that really gets people involved: **contests**. Human beings love competing against each other. Rather than just hold a random drawing for a winner of one of your products or services, make the contest a game of skill, creativity, or knowledge. Sure, it's nice to win something in exchange for nothing, but when you make winning contingent on talent or skill, it is much more memorable.

A contest can also help direct your business. Are you thinking of designing a new logo, offering a new product, or coming up with a fresh tag line? Let others come up with ideas and reward the best one with a prize.

Leverage your contest to its full potential. Promote it heavily before and during the dates it is effective. You can do this online, with an ad in the local newspaper, via printed posters, bulletin board flyers, etc. Make sure that participants know how, when, and where the results will be posted. You might want to require that entrants opt in to your website in order to submit their entries (building your database at the same time) or be present in your store when the announcement is made. Contests can easily drive traffic to an online or offline site and provide numerous ways to use the Law of Multiplication to your advantage.

Public relations are always important, especially for start-ups and local businesses. Your prospective clients will respond favorably when you show an interest in your community, a charity, or a great cause associated with your industry. **Sponsoring** an event or fund raiser is an excellent way to give back while earning you the opportunity for selfless promotion via your company name and logo on all the event's collateral.

Is your marketing budget strapped for cash? A sponsorship doesn't necessarily require you spend money. If your company distributes bottled beverages, why not supply cold drinks for free at the end of a marathon? You could volunteer time to help a charitable organization with an event such as sponsoring a food drive at Christmas with a box to collect items in your store or office.

Another type of sponsorship to consider is **placement ads**. This refers to strategic placement of your products where they are likely to be seen, such as in a movie or television show. Chances are you don't have the marketing budget to pitch your product's placement to MGM or CBS, but placement advertising can be accomplished on a much smaller scale. Consider this example. Your company produces a new, healthy fruit drink and your marketing goal is to increase brand awareness. Why not ask keynote speakers to keep a bottle on the podium at conferences or sports games announcers to place one in the window of their broadcast booth? This is still placement advertising, albeit more localized.

Does your company have an anniversary coming up? Perhaps you can celebrate your millionth customer or a sales award given to your business by a manufacturer or distributer with an event open to the public. Maybe a celebrity associated with your industry is being featured in a new movie, producing a new product or receiving an award. Any type of **celebration** or **special event** is perfect for involving the community and your customer base as well as giving you face time with them. Throwing a big party is a sure way to attract attention and make lots of prospects aware of your brand.

The thrifty way to celebrate is to pick a Saturday or weekday evening and invite anyone and everyone to visit your store or office. Provide appetizers (fairly cheap when you use the deli at your local grocery store) and beverages or even just hot dogs and sodas; hand out promotional items and draw names for a grand prize (make the entry form an opt in to receive future communications). If you can team up with other businesses and ask them to provide prizes in exchange for promo, it's even cheaper.

A special event is most effective when you use prior promotion to get a big buzz going. Make it something that people eagerly anticipate; offering a mystery prize worth a substantial amount of money is a good way to keep the buzz going.

Some simple ways to promote your event are: adding a small blurb to your sales receipts, including a printed invitation in each fulfilled order, placing posters in your store windows, distributing flyers throughout the community, emailing invitations and day-of reminders to your database. Hype it up and expect a great turnout.

Remember that any kind of promotion will result in sales, and ultimately profits, due to increased familiarity with and confidence in your brand.

Broadcasting

Broadcasting promotionally does not necessarily mean sending a broad message to a broad market; rather it refers to the various ways you can get your marketing message across using the media.

It all starts in your office, whether that's at home or in a commercial building. Have you carefully considered what your **voice mail/on hold message** says to someone calling your company? This is another advertising opportunity that is often wasted. Instead of endlessly looping a recording of your company's virtues, twist the message so that it answers the caller's question of "What's in it for me?"

I know the owner of an audio visual company who uses different phone numbers on advertising directed at different market segments. The on hold/voice mail message is unique to each. So if someone calls in on the line for meeting services, the message reminds the caller to consider new products only his company can provide or to schedule a walk-through with one of his A/V techs in advance of their event. Instead of wasting the time telling the caller how big and great his company is, he uses the opportunity to present a value proposition.

One thing that really works well for branding and promoting small businesses is to become a celebrity of sorts. Particularly in smaller towns, anyone who appears in or on various media receives the benefit of being viewed as an authority figure. This is especially important for entrepreneurs who own a service business such as an attorney, doctor, dentist, accountant, etc. You don't want your taxes done by someone who learned bookkeeping through Peachtree software last week or a doctor to perform a heart transplant if they don't stay abreast of the latest medical innovations, do you? Promotion via media shows consumers that you have the knowledge, experience, and training that make you the perfect person to provide a particular service.

How can you turn yourself into an authority? Through writing a **newspaper column**, preparing a weekly **radio show,** or partnering with a local **television** station to present a regularly scheduled segment.

Here in Phoenix, there are several small business owners who have become local celebrities due to their regular appearances on the morning show of an independent station. One owns a landscaping company and presents a weekly segment on gardening; the other is known as the go-to gal for household cleaning questions and concerns. Both have written books and parlayed their television appearances into broader fame – and lucrative sponsorship contracts. And anyone can do it! Pastors can write a weekly column about the Bible for the newspaper; investment consultants can air a daily radio show covering stock exchange activity; a general contractor can pitch a weekly TV segment teaching viewers how to accomplish small DIY tasks around the house. Think about what topics you will cover and email your pitch with a list of segments to the appropriate person in charge of the features department at your local newspaper office, radio or television station.

Even a single interview with a newspaper or TV reporter can have widespread results. Send a press kit as way of introduction, then follow up with a phone call to the reporter and finish with an appointment to meet face-to-face. Establishing a personal relationship first will greatly enhance your chance of getting featured.

Another benefit of this relationship? Any time a story associated with your specialty is going to print or airing on TV, guess who'll get the call when a professional opinion is needed? Of course it's going to be the person the reporter already knows – and it gives you just one more opportunity to be in the public eye.

Teaching & Training

There's another way to become known as an authority in your industry and that is to share your knowledge with others: teach them, train them, offer valuable information, demonstrate the uses of your products.

Consider those companies that use in-store **product demonstrations** to peddle their wares. How many EZ choppers do you think they sell just by setting up a display in a home goods store with someone chopping vegetables and stir frying them into a mouth-watering concoction right in front of the consumers' eyes?

I've even seen product demonstrations done at swap meets – and scores of customers walking out with the item in tow. This could also be used at craft fairs, festivals, grand opening events, or community yard sales. Of course, tie your product directly into the venue. Do you sell book lights or eBook readers? Ask the owner of a local bookstore if you can set up a demonstration table near the cash register. Maybe you offer athletic shoes. Partner with the local gym to show off the benefits of your shoes directly to those consumers who will be interested in purchasing them.

Things don't always go right with product demonstrations. Consider the young entrepreneur who made a pitch to the City of Seattle for his "Traf-o-data" device which was supposed to automate data processing for traffic sensors. It didn't work when it was supposed to and the 17-year-old was crushed, yelling, "Mom! Come and tell them that it worked!" The young entrepreneur's name? None other than Bill Gates.

Free **training courses**, **seminars**, and **how-to workshops** are another way to promote your brand and products or services. Home Depot and Michael's stores are two companies that use this methodology very effectively by hosting weekly classes. You can bet that when someone leaves a scrapbooking workshop or a landscaping seminar they go shopping first and load up on the necessary supplies. If you do this regularly, you can compile a pretty hefty database and send out monthly calendars showing upcoming events – a very efficient yet free way to ensure that your workshop is well-attended.

Of course these days you don't need to host these types of events in person. It's quite easy to create and present a training seminar via a conference call or online **webinar**. This works particularly well for a company that offers software, consulting services, educational courses, or any type of business tool. The biggest consideration in deciding between a **teleseminar** and a webinar is how important visual aids are to the presentation. If you are considered an expert in your field and you want to showcase an interview or just offer advice, a teleseminar is a good option. However, if you wish to demonstrate the features of an information product or business tool, a webinar is the better choice.

No matter which format you choose, you are bound to get the best results if you promote heavily ahead of time and tease an exclusive, special offer. At the end of the presentation, allow participants to buy the product for a discount available only for a limited time afterward (this is also a highly effective way to increase sales after a speaking engagement). A special offer really compels people to act immediately.

If the first webinar or teleseminar is successful, plan more. Why let the time and effort you've put into a single presentation go to waste? You can re-air it as a recording and reach even more people at no additional cost.

Tip: You really have to promote your teleseminar or webinar ahead of time in order to ensure it is well-attended. Use an automation tool such as Infusionsoft to send a handful or so of promotional emails to your existing database or a purchased list in the week preceding the event. Get people excited about it while piquing their interest – don't tell them exactly what to expect but do focus on the benefits of your product or service.

Branding and promotions are only effective when they uphold your company's marketing objectives and goals. The key is to create a campaign unified by your brand. Robert Evens, chairman of Promotion Marketing Association of America, asks, "Does the consumer really know who you are, or are they buying the brand that is being promoted this week?" Consistency is perhaps more vital for branding and promotional advertising as it for other forms of marketing.

Chapter Seven: Print – Not Just Black & White

"Never write an advertisement which you wouldn't want your family to read. You wouldn't tell lies to your own wife. Don't tell them to mine." – David Ogilvy

There's not much advertising you can't accomplish with a printer (either computer hardware or a printing service). Just look at all these low-cost forms of print mad ads perfect for small businesses:

1. Brochures
2. Catalog
3. Flyers
4. Posters
5. Door hangers
6. Newspaper ad
7. Magazine ad
8. Press Release
9. Classified ad
10. Newsletter ad
11. Yellow pages
12. Coupon Decks/Books
13. Receipts, printing on back of
14. Books
15. Newspaper/ Magazine article
16. Hotel Directories
17. Business Directory
18. Brochure Rack/Rack Cards

Print advertising is perhaps the most popular, recognizable form of advertising to most small business owners. From simple flyers which have been used for centuries, to the famous "wish book" catalogs made popular by Sears and JC Penney to the ads in newspapers and magazines, print advertising has a long track record of being an excellent way to market any business.

The first entrepreneur to use print advertising was Benjamin Franklin. A printer by trade at the time, Ben offered book catalogs. Customers were guaranteed that "Those persons who live remote, by sending their orders and money to B. Franklin, may depend on the same justice as if present."

When it comes to print, copy is king. The less your advertisement *looks like* an advertisement, the more it's going to get noticed. Howard Luck Gossage, late owner of the Freeman, Mander, and Gossage advertising agency, reminds us that, "The real fact of the matter is that nobody reads ads. People read what interests them, and sometimes it's an ad." Gossage is famous for his ability to start conversations with consumers and create compelling headlines such as this one praised by advertising great David Ogilvy, "At 60 miles an hour the loudest noise in this new Land Rover comes from the roar of the engine." It's appealing because it says so much about a customer's concerns in just one short sentence. We'll cover more about headlines when we get to print media advertisements.

While I could write a whole book about copy, there are a few key points to keep in mind when you write text for your own advertising pieces.

First and foremost, consider the goal of the piece. Usually this is to make the recipient *do* something. And whatever that call to action, it needs to relate directly to profits. So you might ask someone to pick up the phone and call your office for an appointment, visit your website and opt-in, send you an email to receive a brochure – or all of these things. The message really depends on who's getting it, however; someone who has already done business with your company needs different information than someone who's never heard of you before. Your existing customer base could receive notice of new products or an invitation to attend a workshop – they don't need to receive basic information because they're already buying from you. A new database, on the other hand, needs an introduction. So the copy must compel the reader to take that first step by making the initial contact.

Professional copy writers often use a tried and true formula: AIDA. This stands for Attention, Interest, Desire, Action. Grab attention with a startling or humorous headline, keep interest with informative body text, create desire to own your products or use your services, and then ask the reader very clearly to take a specific action. Usually it is to your advantage to add a deadline that urges immediate action, such as limiting the dates you offer a discount or sale price in a printed ad. In other instances, such as a printed brochure, book, or directory listing, the information needs to be evergreen. Keep in mind the purpose of your marketing as well as the purpose of the specific piece when you sit down to write appropriate copy.

My final piece of copy writing advice is to never talk down to your target market. Don't assume they are stupid and they won't notice there is nothing to back up the claim of your product's quality, popularity, or value. I've lauded Apple for using some truly creative advertisements and personally, I'm a big fan of Apple products. But I ran across a print ad from the early 1980s that shows a picture of Benjamin Franklin with a Macintosh II on his desk (a huge box connected to a tiny television monitor) and a tag line of "What kind of man owns his own computer?" The copy was supposed to convince consumers they needed a computer in their homes through this copy: "It's less expensive than timesharing. More dependable than distributed processing. Far more flexible than centralized EDP. And, at less than $2500 (as shown), downright affordable." Affordable? That's roughly $6,000 to $7,000 in today's dollars. I don't believe this ad did anything to improve Apple's early sales simply because they were underestimating the intelligence of the consumer.

When it comes to writing advertising copy, remember that even graffiti is advertising. The best campaigns, however, are centered on great, succinct tag lines that identify the core attribute of a product or service with strong, interesting, memorable copy.

Although you can't have a great print advertisement without great copy, the visual aspect is important, as well. A powerful image can say a lot without words. Think of the "Got Milk" ads – they feature nothing more than a celebrity with a milk moustache, the famous tag line, and a short paragraph, yet they are extremely successful.

Products Without People

What happens if the product you are advertising in print is prohibited from showing someone using it? If you're a truly creative Mad Man, you come up with a unique way to get around the stumbling blocks.

Take, for instance, Fruit of the Loom underwear. Until the mid-1950s, the company known mainly for producing men's underwear was called Union Underwear due to their most popular product, the union suit. As it changed hands, it became known simply as Fruit of the Loom, a term previously applied to finely woven cloth. Even before the name was taken over by the underwear company, it was closely associated with an apple; with the addition of a leaf and bunch of grapes visuals, Fruit of the Loom really became memorable.

But how do you advertise something as intimate as men's underwear in an era when Ozzie and Harriet had to sleep in separate beds? The advertising agency's solution was to show the fruit instead of the product. Even though our moral standards have now relaxed enough to allow people in underwear to be shown in magazines and during prime time television viewing, the "fruit guys" will be forever linked to Fruit of the Loom.

A similar stumbling block plagued the cigarette industry after the Surgeon General released its report linking smoking to cancer back in the 1960s. Shortly afterward, advertising showing actual people with a cigarette was banned. One intrepid advertising exec thought came up with the idea of a cartoon camel to promote Camel cigarettes. The animal could be shown with a cancer stick hanging out of his mouth and this neatly solved the problem of print ads – although that, too, would later be banned since it was deemed too influential on children.

The moral of the story is that no matter what advertising obstacles are in place, there is always a creative way to get around them. Just as Apple advertised a product without ever showing it, so can you advertise a product without people.

Now let's take a look at the advertising methods that require excellent written copy and strong visuals.

The Basics

I can't think of a single type of business that couldn't benefit from a nice sales **brochure**. It can be a simple trifold you create with your own desktop publishing program or a really unique format such as an oversized vellum envelope tied with a ribbon that opens up to reveal glossy pages in graduated sizes. That unique brochure costs a lot more than the traditional type, though, so it all depends on your marketing budget, your target market, and the purpose of the brochure as to which style you choose. Is it something you want the recipient to retain for a long time? Will it function as a sales letter? Or perhaps you want it to be a mini catalog. Each of these purposes requires a specialized format.

Any brochure needs to include the basic information about your company: logo, tag line, address, contact information, website. But in addition, include copy that shows prospects "What's in it for me?" Tell the reader exactly what you offer and how it fills a need. With a trifold brochure, you've got six pages to work with; don't make it wasted space. Include testimonials, a list of products, photos, a pre-stamped, perforated form for requesting further information, or perhaps a schedule of events. Make it a piece that someone will want to hang on to instead of toss in the trash. And if you're going to spend a large amount of your marketing budget on printing, it's best to keep the information evergreen.

If your business offers products of any kind, a printed **catalog** is a good way to provide something that will be kept around and referred to often. It's been a long time since Sears and JC Penney sent out a big wish book, but that doesn't mean catalogs are no longer popular. In fact, today's specialty retailers often find that printed catalogs sell more merchandise than websites.

Most people I know enjoy receiving a catalog in the mail and thumbing through it looking for items they want or need. This makes a catalog a very effective form of advertising because – unlike a website – it will stay around the home or office for some time.

A really inexpensive form of print advertising is the simple **flyer**. Use your computer and printer to create a nicely designed – but not overly ornate or fussy – page that can be posted almost anywhere. You can canvass a neighborhood and stick them in mailboxes, put them underneath the windshield wipers of vehicles in a parking lot, tack them up on bulletin boards, tape them in store windows, or mail them. You also turn your printed flyer into an Adobe Acrobat file and offer it for download

Before Montgomery Ward and Sears, famed New York jeweler Tiffany & Co. produced a catalog in 1845. It was called a "Catalog of Useful and Fancy Articles" featuring "the largest, richest and best collection of elegant articles of taste and utility to be found on this side of the Atlantic."

through your website. This is a great way to advertise the opening of a new business, a new product, or just create brand awareness in a particular locale.

Posters are really nothing more than a bigger flyer. They work best as a way to promote an important event, such as an artist's showing at a gallery or an upcoming conference with famous (or semi-famous) speakers. Although you can print posters in-house with the right equipment and paper, I recommend that you splurge on professional printing services and perhaps even a graphic artist. Glossy and colorful is preferable to bland and homemade in order for a poster to be noticed.

Door hangers are similar to flyers, too. They should contain the same type of information in a slightly different format and size. Just like flyers, they can be distributed to houses, hung on mail boxes, or placed on the door handles of each business in an office complex. Printing a large quantity is quite inexpensive, but their use is a bit more limited than flyers or business cards. Door hangers work best for service companies wishing to saturate local neighborhoods or business areas.

Print Advertisements

We discussed a bit about writing copy earlier in this chapter by going over the AIDA formula. But the most important feature of an advertisement that runs in a magazine, newspaper, newsletter, or classified section is the headline. If you can't grab 'em with a compelling headline, the odds are slim to none that anyone will read further.

Advertising Hall of Fame inductee Morris Hite explains it this way, "The headline is the most important element of an ad. It must offer a promise to the reader of a believable benefit. And it must be phrased in a way to give it memory value." So, there are the two key components of a great headline: 1) believable benefit; and 2) memorable copy.

The following is a list of "power" words for headlines that I've compiled from a variety of sources:

Absolute	Incredible
Accurate	Ingenious
Advanced	Insider
Advantage	Introducing
Afford	Limited Time
Amazing	Love
Astonishing	Luxury
Awesome	Opportunity
Believe	Massive
Breakthrough	New
Brilliant	Original
Dangerous	Phenomenal
Deluxe	Power(ful)
Discover	Proven
Dramatic	Replenish
Easy	Reveal(ed)
Eco-friendly	Savvy
Effective	Secret
Eliminate	Sexy
Embarrassing	Shortcut
Environmentally Safe	Special
Exciting	Stronger
Experts	Stunning
Free	Success(ful)
Genius	Tips
Hidden	Ultimate
How To	Urgent
Imagine	Win
Improve(d)	Wonder

While by no means comprehensive, this list gives you plenty of headline fodder. In fact, you should be able to combine any of these words and create a really compelling headline for nearly any ad. Have you ever played "Mad Libs" with your kids? These are books that start with one person asking another a series of innocent questions, such as "What is your favorite color?" or "What flavor do you prefer: chocolate or vanilla?" Those answers are then inserted into a prearranged story in the appropriate spots. The resulting story can be hilarious! This same concept can be applied to creating a headline. How about "Amazing Opportunity for a Limited Time" or "Urgent! The Breakthrough Secret You Can't Afford to Miss" or "Insider Secrets for Success". You get the idea. These combinations can be used for any type of business, whether it offers products or services.

Remember to include the basics, too. Believe it or not, I've actually seen a newspaper advertisement for a big, upcoming event that didn't include the date! I'm sure whoever wrote the copy for that one heard about it from the higher-ups right away. And always, always include a call to action. It's not enough to get someone to read the copy. Then what? They put aside the magazine and forget about it? You want them to take action; immediately is preferable.

Print advertisements can be expensive. The larger the circulation of a newspaper, magazine, or newsletter, the more you can expect to pay for space. Advertising in the largest circulation publications is not necessarily the most effective, however. There are some savvy entrepreneurs who have done nothing more than run consistent classified ads at a fraction of the cost of a half page in a big metro newspaper. Of course, the keys to making this work are knowing your target market and writing copy that appeals to them.

Look for specialty publications that correlate with your niche. These usually have much lower distribution numbers, but the readers are more targeted to your message. Do you sell crafting supplies? There are lots of newsletters and magazines devoted specifically to yarn crafts, scrapbooking, homemade décor, and the like. B2B companies can keep costs down by limiting their print advertisements to industry, association, or trade publications whose readers are more likely to be prospective buyers. Don't forget periodicals that focus on human resource professionals, blue collar workers, start-ups, ethnic groups, religious groups, working moms, senior citizens, etc. For every demographic and psychographic there is bound to be a publication that addresses it.

Newsletter ads are a thrifty way to advertise. Complementary small businesses can share databases by exchanging ads in their respective newsletters for free. Even if your partner company is unwilling to do an even exchange, you can probably purchase space in their newsletter for a very small investment. Making this type of ad effective relies on the size of the newsletter's distribution and matching the demographics of its readers.

Press releases provide a means of disguising your advertisements as news. This is a wonderful forum for educating the community about your business while sharing news of an accomplishment, award, event or the like. Press releases can be submitted to newspapers throughout the country (as long as the information is relevant) and to the plethora of online sites that distribute them. There is often a fee for widespread distribution, so be sure that the release is written as an effective advertising piece.

Tip: make sure the release is actually newsworthy if you want it featured in a newspaper. You might want to hire a professional press release writer to ensure your release is slanted as news and not just self-promotion – that might work online but it won't cut the mustard for a nationally syndicated publication.

The final form of print advertisement I recommend for small business owners is ad space in the **Yellow Pages**. A lot of people use the internet to find a company but believe it or not, there are still a few holdouts that use a land line and a physical phone book. Besides, phone books are widely distributed, regardless of whether or not the residence has a home phone number. I know several people who throw a copy of the Yellow Pages in their car so it's always handy when they're out and about. If you can't afford an advertisement, a bolded listing is your next best bet. But do remember that a single ad is valid in the phone book for a year (and also includes an online listing) so you are really only outlaying a twelfth of the entire cost monthly from your marketing budget.

The secret for success with a coupon deck? Ask for the top spot on the stack so your coupon is the first one showing.

More Forms of Printed Advertising

Small business owners have many more options available when it comes to spreading their message through print marketing. The cost is anywhere from free to mid-range; select the ones that make the most sense for your business and its marketing objectives.

Those bundled **coupon decks** and **books** you've probably received frequently in your mailbox represent a relatively inexpensive way to saturate a large portion of a particular city or region. Val Pak is perhaps the largest company that distributes bundled packages of buck slips (so called because they are about the size of a dollar bill). A lot of families – both wealthy and financially strapped – are paying more attention to these coupons now that every penny counts in this depressed economy. It works best for companies that provide a necessity; make the offer afford-able and you're bound to get additional sales from a coupon deck.

A lot of large retail chains print **receipts** with advertising on the back, grocery stores in particular. The way to make them work? Don't use a lot of text. Make your compelling headline stand out and include a simple offer, such as a coupon or freebie, in addition to your phone number and website URL. Any more than that, and it's likely to get trashed without a further thought. The most effective use for an ad on the back of a receipt is to drive traffic to your website – offer an incentive to get action. Another thing to remember? Studies have shown that women tend to look on the back of a receipt; the majority of men just throw it away without a second thought. This could be an effective form of advertising *if it fits your target market.*

Have you ever considered writing your own **book**? I'm not re-ferring to the next *Odyssey* or *Gone With the Wind;* rather a simple workbook, instructional manual, or educational piece. Write what you know about – something that coincides with your business. Don't be afraid to include a few pages sprinkled throughout that advertise your company. Do make it interesting and find someone else who can edit your writing (any avid reader can probably do a decent job); nothing says unprofessional more than typos and grammatical errors.

Self-publishing is easy and not nearly as expensive as you might think when using print on demand (POD) publishers like Lulu and anyone can submit their book for listing on Amazon. Keep costs even lower by using a cardstock cover and stapled binding from a local print shop so you can give away your books for free. This makes the book better than a business card at net-working events since the book is likely to be saved. Multiply its purpose by creating a digital copy in Acrobat file format you can offer as a download on your website.

Another form of advertising disguised as something else is an **article** you write for a newspaper, magazine, or entertainment publication. Reuse, and rewrite, a blog post or article you wrote for an online application; this makes it quick and easy. Submit the article to a printed periodical. You will likely be afforded a short byline to include your company name and website address.

Not only does an article advertise your business, it establishes you as an authority – and you can provide an online link to the article via your website as well as reprint portions in your bro-chure. Writing one article offers a lot of marketing leverage and you might even get paid for it! What other form of advertising can you imagine that could do that?

Hotel and business directories spread the word of your busi-ness to local consumers. Usually the rate for an ad in these directories is reasonable since you are sharing the cost with other advertisers. Call or visit local hotels and business organizations for information on advertising in their directories.

Hotel directories are a great place for local companies to advertise, particularly if they provide business services, food and beverage, an attraction, or entertainment – anything to which travelers might need access during their stay away from home.

Most hotels have racks of brochures, or **rack cards**, available to guests, presenting another opportunity to target travelers looking for something to do or somewhere to eat. Create a design that stands out amidst all the other cards in the rack; use a bright color and a bold headline.

Tip: Go in and speak to the bell staff at the hotel. If you schmooze with them a bit, they will be more likely to distribute your rack card and recommend your business to guests.

Business directories tend to be distributed by a realty office, local Chamber of Commerce, Convention & Visitors Bureau, Welcome Wagon, or other civic organization that targets visitors to your city. Business people from out of town, new residents, guests, and conference attendees are most likely to receive them. If your target market falls into any of these categories, you will surely benefit from a listing in a directory. Increase the odds of gaining a new customer by including a special offer, such as a discount or freebie.

Whatever type of print advertising you choose for your business, take the advice of Howard Luck Gossar and do your best to "start a conversation" with a prospective client via the written copy. Use the knowledge of your target market gleaned from research to answer questions before they are asked, to address needs before they are expressed, and to pique interest before the reader even realizes his disposition to the appeal of the message.

Chapter Eight: Direct Marketing – Hitting the Bull's Eye When Targeting Prospects

"There is no need for advertisements to look like advertisements. If you make them look like editorial pages, you will attract about 50 percent more readers." – David Ogilvy

Few forms of advertisement are as powerful as direct marketing via a number of means such as these:

1. Postcards
2. Personal letters
3. Sales letters
4. Audio/Video (mail)
5. Lumpy packaging
6. Fax messages
7. Text messages
8. Email messages
9. Telemarketing

Direct marketing simply refers to a marketing communication tool that connects a business with targeted prospects through a message that is mailed, emailed, faxed, or texted. It's direct because it goes right to the target market. Instead of mailing a letter to every fifth person in the phone book, direct mail is sent to a specific group, identified by their demographics and/or psychographics. The recipients can be names already on your prospecting list or a brand new list you purchase from a direct mail marketer such as Melissa Data or infoUSA. A specific advertising campaign could target residents of a certain city or area, an age group, homeowners, families, parents, IRS debtors, businesses by SIC code – there are lots of variables you can use to specifically target a certain segment of the population.

Late advertising executive Fairfax Cone explains the effectiveness of direct marketing like this, "There is no such thing as a Mass Mind. The Mass Audience is made up of individuals, and good advertising is written always from one person to another. When it is aimed at millions it rarely moves anyone." This goes right along with the principle I've already mentioned about developing your ads for the one person out of a hundred who is most likely to become a customer.

The most common form of direct marketing is print but other ways of reaching your targeted prospects are continually changing and developing. Text messages are perhaps the newest way to communicate directly with a customer or prospect while fax messaging is on its way out (but don't discount it entirely).

Often the difference between success and ho-hum results is the timing of your direct marketing campaign. If you are mailing a postcard to consumers, shoot for Saturday delivery when most people have time to actually sit down and read through their mail.

If you're sending a text message, avoid the peak business hours of eight to nine in the morning and four to five in the afternoon. Restaurateurs are likely to benefit by sending an email or text message with a coupon code right around lunchtime.

Tip: My friend Shaun Parson is the mastermind when it comes to mobile marketing. If you are interested in learning more about effective text message advertising, refer to the list of Resources in Chapter 11.

There are certain dates you need to keep in mind, as well. Any direct messages you send in the month or two before Christmas are bound to experience heavy competition since this is the largest retail season of the year. Better holidays to target are Mother's Day, July 4th, and Halloween as these are typically holidays when consumers stay home.

Although you can develop database lists yourself and prepare the mailings, I advise you to find a good company that can work with you to achieve your marketing goals while staying within budget. There are just too many rules and regulations governing direct contact with consumers. Not only do direct mail marketers have access to far more names than you ever could, they will prepare your mailers per postal standards and stay within the law as outlined by CAN-SPAM and the Do Not Call Registry. It's always better to be safe than sorry. You don't want to end up damaging your reputation rather than increasing your bottom line.

Direct Mail Marketing

If it fits into an envelope or package, it can be mailed. Nowadays that means nearly anything. And with the U.S. Postal Service's rollout of flat rate priority mail boxes (with the tag line of "If it fits, it ships"), it's very inexpensive to mail packages of several pounds in weight.

Then again, direct mail doesn't even need an envelope if you are sending postcards or self-mailers. Self-mailers are nearly unlimited – as long as you can write on it, you can mail it – and I've seen some very creative examples of using everyday objects to directly target a specific market.

The biggest advantage of direct mail? Many of your competitors have stopped sending it due to increasing first class postal rates and the misconception that online advertising has taken its place. That gives the entrepreneur who uses direct mail a distinct advantage because there are less promotional pieces in the mailbox competing for the recipient's attention. That also means that direct mail is still a very viable form of advertising.

When planning a direct mail campaign, don't underestimate the importance of the written copy. Just like a magazine or newspaper ad, a compelling headline is vital but the body text comes in a close second. Because mailed letters are usually much longer than an ad or text message, you need to pay special attention to breaking it up into readable chunks, using bold, italicized and underlined fonts, and including more than one call to action.

A common form of direct mail is a **postcard**. Write a simple message, use an attention-grabbing graphic such as a humorous or shocking picture on the flip side, and mail it out for just a few cents per piece. However, postcards, due to their limited size, are best to use as a way to stay in touch with existing customers rather than as the first form of contact with a prospect database. Postcards work well for introducing a new product, presenting a special offer, or as an invitation to an event – but not as the initial intro- duction to your company. It takes more space to convince someone to try your business for the very first time than what is available on a postcard.

Have fun designing your postcard. Humor is appropriate for many businesses; be creative about finding an image that works well with a playful headline. I know of a church that did an out- reach mailing with a postcard. On the picture side was a photo of a young boy with a grumpy expression sitting in front of a plate piled high with green peas. On the text side, the headline read "You're not a kid anymore...appease your spirit." This play on words was a real eye-catcher and lent a playful note to a typically serious organization.

If there's any way you can make the time to do so, send out a **personal letter** to anyone inquiring about your business. Hand address the envelope and use a stamp rather than a mail permit imprint so it *looks* like personal correspondence.

You might be surprised at just how effective personal letters are. Can you imagine receiving correspondence from the CEO of Disney Corporation that is not a form letter but a hand-written missive? Wouldn't that make you much more apt to visit Disneyland and spend your money on Disney products? Sure it can be a form letter; the trick is to not make it look like a form letter.

Many companies find that sending **sales letters** is a very effective form of advertising. And it certainly can be, as long as you carefully select your target market. Sales letters can be anywhere from a single page to several; the length of yours depends on what you are selling.

A client of mine, who offers tax lien and deed seminars, uses sales letters with great success. Some of them are 17 pages long! You may think that no one will read that many pages of text, but he writes them so skillfully and breaks up the text with testimonials and calls to action so well that he can fill a huge conference room full of people due to his sales letters alone. Of course, he doesn't stop at the first one. He stays in regular communication with his database. He also includes a photo of himself at the top of each letter so that by the time someone receives several missives, they feel as if they know him personally. I would strongly recommend sales letter as a great way to introduce a company that offers a service.

Movie Marketing Brings a Gift in the Mail

Since the internet exploded and millions of American consumers bought personal computers for instant access to information across the globe, many advertising execs claimed that direct mail marketing was dead. Email moved quicker than postal mail; advertising on the net was considered the vital centerpiece of any marketing plan.

Sure, AOL had great success sending discs with preloaded software across the country. But that was in the 1990s. Who would use direct mail in the 21st century?

The answer: Netflix.

As the 20th century drew to a close, Blockbuster was the king of movie rentals. Reed Hastings wasn't satisfied with their service. He thought it was a true crime to charge patrons late fees when movies weren't returned to the store on time. Hastings decided to open his own competing movie rental service, operating out of a small warehouse in San Jose, California. His movies could be ordered from a consumer's home, sent via mail, and there would be no late fees assessed – a novel idea at the time.

Ever the visionary, Hastings opted to name the business Netflix, rather than Movies by Mail or another moniker that would more aptly describe the company's service.

The first movie to leave the Netflix warehouse under a subscription plan was True Crime.

Since that time, more than a billion movies have been sent to customers' home via the U.S. mail. Advertising via television and the internet propelled the company to quickly surpass Blockbuster's sales. Blockbuster was forced to emulate Netflix's business model but the move came too late. Currently the company is facing bankruptcy and not expected to survive.

Meanwhile, Netflix is still going strong. In response to the new ways that consumers can watch movies online or even via their smartphones, the company changed alongside, offering instant downloads via the internet.

The success of Netflix is not only due to its visionary founder, but to its advertising. Their most brilliant campaigns used movie characters, with spots showing everything from a fairy princess to a military general getting ready to be shipped or appearing in a customer's home.

A great idea + great advertising = massive success.

But remember that direct mail isn't limited to merely postcards and letters. A great way to repurpose audio podcasts or video presentations offered on your website is to burn them onto **CDs** or **DVDs**. Print a nice label for the CD, slip it into a jewel case, and insert a customized sleeve with your company logo and contact information. Most people will pop it into their CD or DVD player for nothing else than the curiosity factor – and getting them to see and hear your message is the first big hurdle in advertising.

Another client of mine, who is an attorney, is a big believer in sending out DVDs. Anyone who makes an inquiry with his office receives a kit in the mail which includes a brochure, letter, business card, and a DVD of the same video greeting he uses on his website. The video goes over what a client should bring to an appointment, what to expect from the initial consultation, and answers the most frequently asked questions from former clients. Not only is this is a great way to market his firm, it eliminates a lot of phone calls from people asking the same questions over and over again. That's true guerrilla strategy!

The package this attorney sends out qualifies as **lumpy packaging**. This term refers to anything you mail that is outside the dimensions of an ordinary envelope. It can be an odd-shaped package or a box, or even the promo item itself with a stamp stuck on the outside. Lumpy packaging is very successful because the recipient sees its value and wants to reciprocate. The curiosity factor works in your favor, too. Could you resist opening a mysterious package personally addressed?

Don't waste the opportunity to use the outside of the package; it can really increase the mystery of what might be contained inside. The "tax lien and deed king" often pastes smiley face stickers all over the outside of the box and hand writes the first name of the recipient on every side. Talk about a real attention getter!

Perhaps the best example of direct mail lumpy packaging is from another one of my clients. He offers business consulting and resources to home service companies (housecleaners, laundry departments, environmental services, etc.). His direct mailer was a small whiteboard, the kind you might post in your kitchen to share messages with family members or use to write a list of needed groceries. The cork side had an address label and several stamps to cover postage; the whiteboard side was a list written with black marker. The list included such things as "pick up dry cleaning", "go shopping", etc. The last item on the list urged increasing profitability by calling his business, along with the phone number. His response rate to this mailer was fantastic – approaching ninety percent!

Whatever you decide to mail, ensure that it fits with your business niche. Some items you could consider mailing are: balsa wood models (a car for an auto repair shop, a motorcycle for a Harley dealer); puzzles (one made from a logo or product picture could be used for any company); makeup samples (cosmetologist or home beauty products representative); bandages (doctor); recipes (kitchen supply or culinary school); or sugar-free gum (dentist). Be creative. Anything small and inexpensive is perfect for accompanying your sales materials and making a package lumpy – thus more likely to get opened.

Direct mail marketing does work, even in this day and age of computers, smart phones, and iPads. There's just something special about receiving a letter or package in the mail addressed to you. Perhaps it plays on our sense of nostalgia for decades past when most communication was sent via the U.S. Postal Service. Can you remember being a youngster and getting a letter in the mail addressed to you and how excited it made you feel? Lumpy packaging certainly uses the law of reciprocity by providing a nifty item for free. It also builds brand recognition. Altogether, direct mail should be a central part of any entrepreneur's marketing plan.

Other Forms of Direct Marketing

Of course you don't need to rely on the postal service to send your marketing message. You can also use the fax machine, email, cell phone, and telephone to get through to prospects.

Fax messages are, honestly, the least effective form of advertising. But I include the option here because it is very inexpensive and could be a boon for a B2B company that wants to stay in contact with an existing client database. You can buy a fax number list from a direct marketing firm but faxes that are unsolicited are apt to make their way directly into the wastebasket, unfortunately. The best use of fax messaging is to inform current customers of new products, invite them to special events, or perhaps pass along a new price list for your products or services.

Email messages can be quite effective but there are several caveats when using this advertising methodology. The very first – and most important – consideration is that you must only send messages to subscribers who have opted in to receive your communication. I've touched on this before but I can't stress too much the importance of being in compliance with the CAN-SPAM laws.

Fortunately, it is relatively easy to get opt-ins. Many companies create a standalone web landing page that is set up purely to obtain opt-in subscribers. I've also mentioned other ways to entice people to opt-in to your communications such as getting their consent on a contest entry, in exchange for a free goody, or even on a business reply card requesting more information.

The second hurdle is creating an email that won't get snagged by the recipient's spam filters. Many people have an email account through their Internet Service Provider (ISP) but use proprietary software, such as Microsoft Outlook, to manage their account. This presents two spam filters: one at the point of delivery through the ISP and one at the point of delivery to the software program. Getting around both can be tricky.

I recommend that the first email you send to a new opt-in not contain any links save for one to your main website in the signature line. Keep the text simple; a "thank you for joining us" message is fine. Forgo fancy designs and graphics. A number of images and website links will ensure that your message goes straight to the spam folder. End the first email message with a reminder to add the sender's address to the list of contacts and/or safe senders. This helps to ensure that future communications get through to the recipient's inbox.

What should your email message do? There are many ways you can use email for advertising. You can create a follow-up sequence that offers a series of informative articles with a call to action such as phoning your office, making an appointment, or buying a product. You could use email to send out a weekly or monthly newsletter. You might want to showcase a new product and include a buy link. You could also send notice of a limited time offer, a special discount, or a coupon code redeemable online. Fit the context of the message into your overall marketing plan along with an appropriate call to action.

Tip: If you are using social media (and you certainly should be), repurpose your Twitter posts. Limited to 140 characters, the same posts make excellent text messages!

Text messaging is very similar to email messaging. The purpose is the same, but you may have to change the call to action. Someone with a smart phone, such as an iPhone, can click on a link in the text message, but others cannot so provide more than one way to satisfy a call to action. You are limited to very short copy, as well, so the message and the call to action must be succinct. Text messaging works wonderfully for advance notice of a special sale, a coupon code, or event invitation; not a way to introduce your company but a way to promote awareness and branding.

The history of tele-marketing goes back to 1903. Multi-Mailing Company of New York was the first to undertake the arduous task of gathering phone books and extracting names and numbers. In New England alone, there were over 600,000 numbers listed! Their specialty was tapping into rural independent telephone lines with 100 subscribers or less – a market that could only previously be reached via traveling salesman (rural post offices were not yet widespread).

Lastly, **telemarketing** is a manner of direct marketing that can be beneficial, if done correctly. Just as email is constrained by CAN-SPAM, telemarketing is limited to consumers who have not placed their phone number on the National Do Not Call Registry. If you purchase a list of phone numbers from a reputable direct marketing firm, you can be assured that the list you receive is clean (also referred to as "list hygiene") – checked against the registry.

Most of us remember when telemarketing was a real nightmare for the average consumer. You would just be sitting down to dinner when the phone rang and invariably it was someone asking you to sign up for a new credit card. That's what prompted the Do Not Call Registry in the first place.

In order to be successful with telemarketing, it needs to be done on a grand scale. It's difficult for someone with a small staff to devote a lot of hours to calling. It is probably more beneficial to hire a telemarketing group that can do the actually calling as well as produce a comprehensive report. This also helps you determine what's working and what isn't, based on the message, time of day, and associated response rate. As with the other methods of direct marketing, focusing on very targeted prospects represents your best bet for success with telemarketing.

Direct marketing in any form is one of the most consistently successful methods of advertising. I recommend making direct marketing the focal point of your plan and using other methodology to augment it.

Chapter Nine: People Connections – Who's Talking About You?

"The work of an advertising agency is warmly and immediately human. It deals with human needs, wants, dreams and hopes. Its 'product' cannot be turned out on an assembly line." – Leo Burnett

Whenever possible, face-to-face and referral connections are the preferred form of mad ads. These are the most powerful methods:

1. Word of mouth
2. Testimonials
3. Endorsements
4. Networking
5. Trade shows
6. Association membership
7. JV/Strategic alliance
8. Affiliate Marketing

Have you ever played that game where one person starts by telling another a story and then that story gets passed around to each successive person in the group? No matter how many times I've played it and no matter the demographics of the participants, the result is always the same: by the time it reaches the last person the message has become so garbled as to be unrecognizable from its initial format.

In advertising, that's not necessarily such a bad thing. Positive publicity has a way of transforming an ordinary achievement into the extraordinary. But there's an opposite side to the coin: the same holds true for negative reviews. Don't ever fool yourself into believing the old adage that "any publicity is good publicity." Especially in today's Web 2.0 world, one negative review can spread virally within hours, or even minutes.

Yes, you want people to talk about you and your company. You want them to spread the story, even if it becomes garbled. Just make sure it's a positive message being passed down.

Bear in mind that your advertising should accomplish what the late publisher and author William Feather so aptly described, "The philosophy behind much advertising is based on the old observation that every man is really two men – the man he is and the man he wants to be." If you can make one man into the person he really wants to be through your products or services, you can bet he's going to spread the word.

Word of mouth advertising is extremely powerful for several reasons. For one, it comes directly from the person who tried your product and service and was very pleased. Average people trust someone like themselves. Secondly, you don't have to do a thing.

165

Word of mouth spreads on its own. This gives you the benefit of not appearing egotistical. If you say your product is great and Joe Blow personally testifies that it is, which do you think carries more weight? And lastly, word of mouth advertising reaches people who are outside your own circle of friends, family, and acquaintances. It drives the marketing car for you and makes lots of stops along the way to visit with friends.

But how can you get word of mouth advertising started? First and foremost, you have to offer a good product or service and stand behind it with exceptional customer service. The average consumer is likely to talk about your business for one of two reasons: he was really blown away by the service, or he was really disappointed, upset, or angry. The only way you can avoid the latter scenario is to do your best to please each and every customer.

One thing I advise every entrepreneur to do is keep track of what people are saying. The sooner you know there's been a negative remark posted about your company, the sooner you can take action to mitigate the damage.

Start by using Google Alerts. If you already have a Google account, simply bring up your personal settings page, click on "Alerts" and input your company name as well as your personal name, surrounded by quotation marks. Any time either appears on the internet, Google will send you an email letting you know where it was posted.

You can do much the same with your Twitter account. If you are using SocialOomph to schedule your tweets, you can schedule alerts that list any tweets posted with @yourname.

These are two of the simplest forms of keeping track of who's saying what about you – and it lets you know if word of mouth advertising is working in your favor.

Celebrity Endorsements Gone Bad

The Beef Industry Council + Cybil Shepherd (she's a vegetarian)

"Got Milk" campaign + the Olsen twins (Mary Kate had an eating disorder)

Hertz Rent-a-Car + O.J. Simpson (enough said)

Testimonials and **endorsements** are two more ways that your company can gain an excellent reputation without you having to toot your own horn. A testimonial is someone saying how wonderful your business is while an endorsement comes from a person who recommends your product or service to others.

Of course, celebrities are the most sought after for providing a testimonial or endorsement. Who wouldn't prefer to use the makeup that Drew Barrymore wears or eat the cereal Michael Phelps does before entering a swimming competition?

But you don't have the Madison Avenue budget to pay a celebrity big bucks to try out your product. Nor do you need to.

Anyone your target market can identify with is fair game. It might be the mayor in your town, an industry icon, or even the curling champion from 1996. As long as it's someone familiar to the consumers you are targeting, a testimonial or endorsement from someone just "kind of famous" is perfectly all right.

Nor is there anything wrong with asking a current satisfied customer to provide an endorsement. Particularly if this is someone who is well-known in the industry, a positive blurb could sway others to give your company a try.

Once you've gotten a written agreement to use a testimonial or endorsement, don't be shy about adding it to your sales collateral, your website, even your email signature. LinkedIn is a great place to add testimonials and the site even allows you to ask for recommendations. It's a potent form of advertising that almost always works wonders for your bottom line because it is based on one of the laws of human nature: we want what others have.

Networking is something any small business owner can do with a great deal of success. It doesn't matter if you're naturally shy. It doesn't matter if yours is a B2C business and not a B2B company. It doesn't matter if you don't have the budget to attend a huge trade show. Networking can be accomplished any time, any place, anywhere.

Trade show participation gives you a unique opportunity to showcase your company to a captive audience. Participants attend specifically to find new products, services, and vendors. The downside is the cost. Between travel, lodging, meals, booth rental, collateral, giveaways, screens and banners, the cost can quickly get out of hand. A less expensive alternative to having your own booth is to partner with your local Convention & Visitors Bureau or other association that might be attending the trade show. You have to share the space but you also get to share the costs.

Trade shows require quite a bit of preparation to give you a good return on investment. Not only do you have to get your own collateral and exhibit supplies in place, you should spend time contacting the attendees and your current customer database beforehand. The more appointments you can set up prior to the event, the greater your chances of turning the trade show into a success.

Trade shows are an excellent place to get new sales from existing clientele as well as finding new customers interested in your products or services. And it doesn't end after all the exhibits have been taken down and packed up. Back at the office, leverage those new contacts you made by communicating with them on a regular basis. Remind them of your introduction at the event and continue the relationship. Sales might not come immediately but they are bound to be a real possibility in the future.

Networking closer to home is a viable option for any small business owner on a Main Street budget. Join as many organizations and **associations** as you can. Most cities have a Chamber of Commerce that welcomes any member of the community for a nominal annual fee. There are bound to be associations related to your industry and many more local networking organizations that fit into your budget. Attending regularly scheduled events is a great way to inform community members about what your business provides. Schmoozing with your fellow association members can often lead to referrals – maybe not immediately but sometime in the future. If you make a commitment to attend as many functions as possible, you become more familiar and you are bound to be the first name that comes up when someone needs your products or service.

While it's always good to attend weekly or monthly events and socialize, you don't have to if the thought makes you cringe. Usually one of the benefits of membership is access to the organization's database. Use it. Not everyone on the list is a competitor; some could easily become **joint ventures** or a partner in a **strategic alliance**.

A joint venture is an agreement between two businesses to work toward a common goal. It could involve a product that is mutually produced, a service that is provided by one partner and marketed by the other, or an even exchange of sales leads. When it comes to advertising and profitability, two entities striving for the same goal are often better than one.

If you really want to use the law of multiplication to grow your business, consider bringing on **affiliate marketers**. These are people whom you agree to give a percentage of the sales price or profits in exchange for promotion; alternately you can also pay them per click through to your website via a unique URL. One company I use, and probably the best referral network in the country, is www.icon.dsadvocates.com/prelaunch. There are many people online now who do nothing but affiliate marketing and earn a good living from it. They know the ins and outs of internet marketing, how to drive traffic, and how to get click-throughs to your offer.

And the Band Played On...and On

Getting someone else to promote and sell your products for a share of the profits isn't a new idea. It's been going on for a long time, particularly in the music industry. Decades ago, Columbia House and BMG had a thriving mail order business selling cassette tapes and CDs. Their growth was largely accomplished through incentivizing their customers. For every "friend" you signed up on the service, you received a certain number of CDs free. This could be considered one of the earliest forms of affiliate marketing.

When businesses starting moving online, so did Columbia House and BMG, but not until after CDNow came onto the scene.

Started in 1994 as a basement operation by twin brothers Jason and Matthew Olim, CDNow used a drop-ship system to take and fulfill orders for music CDs and videos. The enterprising brothers rode the heyday of the dotcom boom, growing by leaps and bounds and quickly expanding beyond their garage operation.

Although the company couldn't survive the dotcom bust, CDNow is credited with creating the first online affiliate marketing program outside of the adult industry (namely Cybererotica). The process was simple: they traded links for kickbacks. The first affiliate marketer to sign on with CDNow was Geffen Records. Back then, there was no way to track where online sales came from other than the arduous task of looking through the path of the click-through.

Since then, other etailers began to use the affiliate marketing model to increase sales, Amazon being the biggest. In 2000, Amazon copyrighted an affiliate management software program. Now, it's quite common to find companies of all kinds offering affiliate marketing programs. But it wasn't until a pair of brothers in a Pennsylvania basement operating on a Main Street budget came up with a truly unique way to advertise that the model we now know and use was officially born.

Whether or not affiliate marketing is a good option for your business depends on its size. Affiliate marketers can get some pretty decent payouts through larger, financial- or legal-based service companies, such as loan modification firms, lawyers, mortgage lenders, and the like. You have to make it worth their while to really push promotion of your products or services. Then again, you could solicit someone who is new to affiliate marketing – perhaps even a friend or family member – and work with a sliding scale for payment. The advantage is that the affiliate doesn't get paid unless you get a sale. Determine if affiliate marketing makes sense for your business and go from there.

Never bypass the opportunity to use human resources for advertising. Ask your satisfied customers to provide testimonials and encourage word of mouth publicity. Let anyone who is an ardent advocate of your business know that you appreciate their efforts; a bit of ego-stroking helps them feel good about continuing and might just encourage others to do the same. The better you get at networking, the more opportunities you will find in places you might not expect. Every contact with a person is a potential sale.

Chapter Ten: Five More Creative Ways to Advertise Your Small Business

"In advertising, not to be different is virtual suicide." – William Bernbach

There's still a handful of creative mad ads that are effective but don't quite fit in with other categories. They are:

1. Surveys
2. Remarketing
3. Table Tops
4. Board/Video Games
5. Movie theatre ads

These advertising extras are not just afterthoughts. They are creative ways to further expand your marketing reach and excellent adjuncts to your overall marketing plan – just some of the ways you can think outside the box when it comes to advertising.

Surveys are included as a form of advertisement because they increase awareness of your company and its brand. When you send a survey to your customers and prospects, it lets them know you value their opinion. It also indicates that you are striving to make your business better, based on the comments from the people who patronize it.

Surveys are easy to create yourself for a small database. They can be printed and mailed, emailed, or provided online for anonymity. If you are asking for sensitive information or mailing the survey to a large group, you may want to enlist the services of a professional research company.

As you have probably learned by now though, you can utilize a survey for more than just promoting good will. In conjunction with a contest, a survey is an excellent way to determine if a new product will be well received by your customers or get their opinion on a proposed change before it is instituted. Surveys are also a great way to gather data for your target market research; the more questions you ask, the greater detail you can add to the demographics and psychographics of your customers.

One way to develop renewed interest in your products or services is by **remarketing** them. The term remarketing applies to any way that you advertise the same offerings or target the same market more than once. So, for instance, with a Google Adwords PPC campaign, you can remarket to visitors who have previously clicked through to your site and highlight a particular product you want them to view. This allows repeated exposure to the same group to greatly increase brand awareness and confidence.

Remarketing can also be used for any product or service that is experiencing declining sales. If you've got an item that was once in high demand but sales are flagging due to any number of changing factors, remarketing it with a slant toward overcoming current buying objections could breathe new life into the product's popularity. Remember the story of Volkswagen reintroducing its Beetle? The manufacturer timed this remarketing effort perfectly, advertising its fuel efficiency and aiming the new bug at consumers who fondly remembered the old bug of the Mad Men era.

In the chapter on signage, I prompted you to think about places you could put your marketing message that are unexpected – high, low, and everywhere in between. But have you ever thought about placing your ad on a **table top**? Personally, I've seen several examples of this. There are restaurants that laminate a page full of ads to the surface of dining tables as well as pubs that have done the same thing on the bar. Just think of all the places where the public gathers and you can find a table: airports, bus depots, community centers, libraries, shopping malls, and many more. If you can think of a venue that would reach your target market and there's no table top advertising currently in place, gather a few of your co-business owners together and put together a proposal. Few places wouldn't at least consider this option since it brings them unexpected incremental revenue.

If you really want to engage your target market, consider creating a **board or video game** based on your company and its industry. Many famous brands have capitalized on their popularity by doing this; think of Tony Hawk's skateboarding video game or the New York Giants' version of Monopoly. There are even companies that specialize in creating a customized game for your brand. This is a really unique promo item for giveaways but it can also be sold through your website or brick-and-mortar store for incremental revenue.

Make this advertising concept even more fun for your customers by hosting a competitive game day or posting high scores online. People love a challenge and the more time they play your specially branded game, the more apt they are to remember your company when it comes time to make a purchase.

The final creative advertising idea is running an ad on a **movie theater** screen. Surprisingly affordable, advertisements aired on the big screen before the start of a movie can also be very effective. I know I've gone to the theater early on many occasions, particularly when the movie is a blockbuster and prone to selling out, and spent half an hour or more watching the ads before the main feature started. After all, there's nothing else to do so these ads are shown to a captive audience.

The demographics of movie watchers are very diverse so it's rather difficult to hit your target market in a theater. Then again, that might be an excellent question to add to a survey: How many times a month do you watch a movie at the local theater? It's an innocuous question that could really help you determine where best to spend your advertising dollars.

Now that you've gotten a detailed overview of the 107 mad ads for any small business, you should have a good idea of what methods you'd like to try based on how best to reach your target market. In the final chapter, I'll give you examples of excellent campaigns for any business depending on the size of its marketing budget. Following that is a list of all the methods presented in this book. I hope you've taken notes along the way; the final step for your business is adding all these mad ads into your marketing plan.

I hope you've enjoyed the journey! Have a great trip as you implement these no-cost and low-cost ways to advertise, brand, and position your business – and give the big companies with their big Madison Avenue agencies a run for their money.

Chapter Eleven: Mad Ads for Any Size Budget and the Necessary Resources

"We didn't actually overspend our budget. The allocation simply fell short of our expenditure." – Keith Davis, football player

Earlier in this book we went over the basics of a marketing plan, including the budget. I recommended that you allocate somewhere around ten percent of your gross sales for advertising. For some companies, that's a healthy amount while for others it can be rather slim. The good news is that no matter how small your budget, there's an effective advertising campaign you can put in place to help increase those profits.

Each business is unique. Only you can determine what factors affect your sales, such as seasonal changes, economic conditions, price sensitivity, and the like. The examples of annual advertising campaigns I include in this chapter are just that – a rough estimate of what you absolutely need along with additional advertising methods which will probably benefit your company.

Take a look through these examples and see which ones you can use in your own business.

Small Retail Business

< $100,000 in annual sales /
10% budget allocation
Essentials:
- Website
  o Products
  o Shopping cart/upsells
  o Blog
  o RSS feed
  o PPC
- Social media
- Online directory
- Business cards
- Coupons
- Catalog
- Yellow Pages
- Newspaper ad
- Text messaging
Optional
- Facebook ad
- Shopping cart ad
- Public restroom
- Banners
- Special events
- Demonstrations
- Coupon deck
- Magazine ad
- Hotel directory
- Table top ad

< $1,000,000 in annual sales /
10% budget allocation
Essentials:
All the same plus
- Sponsored links
- Opt-in
- Auto responder sequence
- Article Directories
- Webinars/Seminars
- Book
- Testimonials
- Networking
- Newsletter
Optional
- Television appearance
- Radio show
- TV segment
- Press releases
- Strategic alliance
- Affiliate marketing
- Games
- Screens & banners

Mid-Sized Service Business

The 107 Mad Ads Methods for Main Street Budgets

Online

1. Website
2. Search Engine Optimization (SEO)
3. RSS feeds
4. Video
5. Link exchange
6. Sponsored link
7. Opt-ins
8. Auto responder sequence
9. eBooks
10. Blog
11. Social Bookmarking
12. eBrochure
13. eGreeting cards
14. Game
15. Forum
16. Online Contest
17. Online Survey
18. Podcasts
19. Shopping Cart upsells
20. Social Media
21. Social Groups
22. Viral/Referral Marketing
23. Facebook ads
24. Pay-per-click (PPC)
25. Guest blogging
26. E-zine
27. Article Directories
28. Bulletin / Message Boards
29. Online Business Directories
30. Webinars
31. iPhone / Smart Phone Apps

Signage

32. Graphic Wraps
33. Digital Menu Boards
34. Shopping cart ads
35. Public Restrooms
36. Bulletin Boards
37. Billboards
38. Banners
39. Spinners
40. Sandwich Boards
41. Park Bench
42. Bus

43. Cabs
44. Mobile billboards (trucks)
45. Vehicle Magnets or Wraps
46. Yard Signs
47. Hot air balloons, blimps, planes

Branding/Promo

48. Business Cards
49. Coupons
50. Screens
51. Promotional Items/ Advertising Specialty
52. Shirts, hats, clothing
53. Free samples
54. Bundling (add to packaged item)
55. Contests
56. Sponsorship
57. Placement ads
58. Special events / Celebrations
59. Voice mail message
60. Local TV appearance
61. Newspaper column
62. Radio show
63. Demonstrations
64. Training courses
65. Free Seminars
66. How To workshops
67. Teleseminars

Print

68. Brochures
69. Catalog
70. Flyers
71. Posters
72. Door hangers
73. Newspaper ad
74. Magazine ad
75. Press Release
76. Classified ad
77. Newsletter ad
78. Yellow pages
79. Coupon Decks / Books
80. Receipts, printing on back of
81. Books
82. Newspaper / Magazine article
83. Hotel Directories
84. Business Directory
85. Brochure Rack/Rack Cards

Direct Marketing

86. Postcards
87. Personal letters

88. Sales letter
89. Audio / Video (mail)
90. Lumpy packaging
91. Fax messages
92. Text messages
93. Email messages
94. Telemarketing

People Connections

95. Word of mouth
96. Testimonials
97. Endorsements
98. Networking
99. Trade shows
100. Association membership
101. JV / Strategic alliance
102. Affiliate Marketing

Further Reach

103. Surveys
104. Remarketing
105. Table Tops
106. Board / Video Games
107. Movie theatre ads

Resources

Online Advertising

Website Hosting and Domain Names

- Go Daddy – Affordable website hosting and domain name registration. Website Tonight application walks you through the quick development of a website.
  http://www.Godaddy.com

- Dot 5 Hosting – Low cost, great customer support, and comprehensive business packages.
  http://www.Dot5Hosting.com

- WordPress – Don't sign up for the free account; buy your domain name and hosting from Go Daddy or Dot 5 first, then install a WordPress platform to create your site. More information and tons of templates available at the site.
  http://www.wordpress.com

RSS Feeds

To find the RSS feed URL for your site, bring it up online. In your browser toolbar, go to View/Page Source. Do a search for "RSS". You should find a line that looks like this:
<link rel="alternate" type="application/rss+xml" title="Example" href=http://www.davidtfagan.com/blog/feed/>
Your RSS feed URL is after href=, in this case:
http://www.davidtfagan.com/blog/feed/

Creating Video Content

- Animoto – Easily make your own slide show with photos, video clips, and music. www.animoto.com

- YouTube – Tutorial: How to Make a Video on YouTube. http://www.youtube.com/watch?v=3zFePU1uvtc

- Video Maker – Video making tips. http://www.videomaker.com/youtube/

Keyword Tools (for good SEO)

- Google Ad Words – Create an account, but there is no need to pay unless you want to start a PPC campaign. http://www.google.com/AdWords

- Word Stream – SEO products and free keyword suggestion tool. http://www.wordstreamcom

Blog Finders (for guest posting, commenting, or link exchanges):

- Fast Blog Finder – Find dofollow and nofollow blogs by keyword. http://www.fastblogfinder.com/

- Word Tracker – Find blogs; also suggests keywords for good SEO. http://www.wordtracker.com/

Opt-ins and Auto Responder Sequences

- Infusionsoft – Fully featured, powerful Email marketing and CRM software. http://www.infusionsoft.com

- Constant Contact – Email marketing, online surveys, and event marketing. http://www.constantcontact.com

Create your own eBook

You can certainly create your own using word processing software and turning it into an Adobe Acrobat file, but if you need help with formatting and distribution, consider a self-publishing service provider.

- Lulu –The number one self-publishing resource; comprehensive self-publishing service that provides an ISBN, formatting guidelines, and distribution to online bookstores such as Amazon. Also prints books. http://www.lulu.com

- Megazine – Turn your eBook into a flip book, a digital version of a book that lets you turn the pages. http://www.megazine3.de

Social Bookmarking

- Del.icio.us - http://del.icio.us
- Digg - http://www.digg.com
- Reddit - http://reddit.com
- Furl - http://www.furl.net
- Stumbleupon - http://www.stumbleupon.com

- Socializer 2.0 – Allows you to submit to several social bookmarking sites at once. http://ekstreme.com/socializer/

- Add This – Provides buttons to add to your website to make it easy for visitors to share your content with others. Also includes sharing analytics program. http://www.addthis.com/

eGreeting Cards

- Custom Sign Generator – Create just about any type of custom graphic, logo, image, cartoon, card, or banner with the tools on this site. http://www.customsigngenerator.com/

- Text 2 Pic – Digital photo mashup site aggregation. http://www.txt2pic.com/

Online Games

- FPS Creator – Create your own first person shooter games. http://www.thegamecreators.com

- RPG Maker – Create your own real player game. http://www.rpgmakerweb.com/

- The RPG Maker Resource kit – Forum, resources, help. http://crankeye.com

- Flash Promo – Order a customized game for your website (UK). http://www.flashpromo.com/

Online Forum for your Website

- vBulletin – Community software. http://www.vbulletin.com/

- BuddyPress – Easy to add community platform for WordPress. http://buddypress.org/

- Yahoo – You can also create a free Yahoo! Group page. http://groups.yahoo.com

Online Surveys

- Survey Monkey – Free and Pro plans available to add a survey to your website. http://www.surveymonkey.com/

- There are free survey widgets available for your blogging platform, too. Check out http://www.wordpress.com or http://www.blogger.com

Podcasts

- About.com – Tutorial on how to create your own podcast (really requires nothing more than a computer with speakers and recording capability). http://radio.about.com/od/createyourownpodcast/ss/How-to-Create-Your-Own-Podcast-Make-Your-Own-Talk-Show-Music-Program-or-Audio-Stream.htm

- iTunes – How to create your own podcast and submit it to the iTunes library. http://www.apple.com/itunes/podcasts/specs.html

Shopping Cart software:

- PayPal – Provides comprehensive business services including shopping cart, credit card merchant services, invoicing. Perhaps the most widely used software on the World Wide Web. https://merchant.paypal.com/cgi-bin/marketingweb?cmd=_render-content&content_ID=merchant/home&nav=2

Check with your web hosting service provider. Most have shopping carts you can add to your website. The software should also include an option for upsales software.

Online Advertising

- Facebook – CPC and CPM options.
  http://www.facebook.com/advertising/

- Hulu – Option advertising; choose from a variety of Ad Experience packages that allow viewers to customize content. http://www.hulu.com/about/advertising/adexperience

- EVB (Evolution Bureau) – Creative technologists that create brand-building interactive advertising such as Elf Yourself and Mistletoe Makeover. http://evb.com/

Article Directories

- eZine Articles – Top-ranked article directory site online with tons of traffic. http://www.ezinearticles.com

- Suite 101 – You have to apply for position as expert on a particular topic. http://www.suite101.com

- Articles Base – Number two ranked (behind eZine Articles). Articles are offered for free use.
  http://www.articlesbase.com/

Message Boards for your Website

- Website Toolbox – Easily add a message board to your website. http://www.websitetoolbox.com/message_board/

- Buddy Press also provides a message board option (see Online Forum Resources)

Online Business Directories

- Yahoo! Local – Add your business to a locality.
  http://local.yahoo.com/
  - o For national or global listing, visit
    https://ecom.yahoo.com/dir/submit/intro/

- Local D – Business directories by locality.
  http://www.locald.com/

- Google Business Directory -
  http://www.google.com/Top/Business/

Yellow Pages online listing is included with your print ad in the phone book.

Webinars

- Webex – Create and host your online event for up to 25 people at a time. http://www.webex.com

- Go To Meeting – Plan, present, and record your webinar. Free accounts with the capability to host larger virtual meetings. http://www.gotomeeting.com/fec/

iPhone and Smartphone Apps

Done For You
- Appiction – http://www.appiction.com
- Gen XM – http://genxm.com

DIY
- MS Mobiles - http://msmobiles.com/article.php/27.html

Graphic wraps

Check with your local printing company – most these days offer graphic wraps for vehicles, buildings, backdrops, windows, etc.

- Rage Wraps – Vinyl wraps for any type of application. http://www.ragewraps.com

- Wrapit Advertising Group – Creates wraps for bathroom stalls and elevators. http://www.wrapitadgroup.com/

Shopping Cart Ads

- Northeast Advertising Corporation – Works with New England supermarkets. http://neadcorp.com

- Cartvertising – Located in Texas; deals with a wide variety of local supermarkets. http://www.cartvertising.com

Check directly with your local grocery stores for opportunities in your locale.

Rest Room Stall Advertising

- Stall Mall – Has advertising opportunities in most major metropolitan areas throughout the U.S. http://www.stallmall.com

Billboards

- Lamar Outdoor – Creates signs for park benches, buses, digital billboards, etc. http://www.lamaroutdoor.com

- Outdoor Billboard – Find billboard space for rent or buy your own. http://www.outdoorbillboard.com

- Clear Channel – One of the biggest billboard advertising companies. Also provides advertising options in airports, taxis, malls, and bike racks. http://www.clearchanneloutdoor.com/

Outdoor Advertising

- Displays 2 Go – Prints sandwich boards, flags, umbrellas, sidewalk and outdoor posters and much more. http://displays2go.com

- National Mobile Billboards – Full service provider for dynamic vehicle signage. http://www.nmbmedia.com/default.aspx

- Skinz Wraps – Provides vehicle wraps as well as bus, taxi, and limo graphic wraps. http://www.skinzwraps.com

Aerial Advertising

- Aerial Media Services – Advertising with any type of aerial vehicle (blimps, balloons, planes). http://www.aerial-media.com/

- Thirty Thousand Feet – Directory of aviation specialists who provide advertising in the sky. http://www.thirtythousandfeet.com/aerialad.htm

- Vista Print – Offers large and small vehicle magnets at a reasonable price (sometimes free!). http://www.vistaprint.com

Branding and Promotion

Promo Items

- Vista Print – Always offers free business cards with their logo on the back side but you can get it removed for a small price. They also print promotional items, clothing, and hats. http://www.vistaprint.com

- Advertising Specialty Services – Offers a full line of promotional products including food, calendars, awards, etc. http://www.adspecialityservices.com

Coupons

- You can easily create your own coupons or use your local printer. For templates and professional printed coupons, try Ticket Printing - http://www.ticketprinting.com/Coupons/.

Screens and Banners

- Pop Up Stands – A full line of trade show advertising items - including banners, screens, table stands, etc. http://www.popupstands.com

Promotion

- Frugals – Bundled packages available for print, online, email, and radio advertising in conjunction with their online site and magazine. http://www.frugals.biz

List of local TV Stations

- Station Index – Comprehensive listing of stations in local markets. http://www.stationindex.com/tv/

List of local Radio Stations

- Radio Locator – Comprehensive listing of radio stations by ZIP code or call letters. http://www.radio-locator.com/

Teleseminars

- Great Teleseminars – Packages include recording, CD master production, and broadcast of your teleseminar. http://www.greatteleseminars.com/

Print

General Printing

- Vista Print – Tons of items, some loss leaders offered for free. Look professional at a low cost. http://www.vistaprint.com

- 48 Hour Print – Need your catalogs, brochures, and other items in a hurry? Get your items printed in two days. http://www.48hourprint.com

- FedEx Kinkos – If you've got a storefront nearby, you can quickly and easily send your files online and pick them up the next day. They offer everything from banners to calendars to bound books. http://www.fedex.com/us/office/

Newspapers Ads

- US Newspapers – Comprehensive listing of local newspapers by state. http://www.usnpl.com/

- Penny Saver - http://www.pennysaverusa.com/local-classified-ads-w-us.html

- Thrifty Nickel – http://thenickel.com

Magazine Ads

- Mondo Times – Comprehensive listing of local magazines and media contacts by state. http://www.mondotimes.com/world/usa.html

Trade Publications

- Wikipedia – Good list of trade magazines and journals. http://en.wikipedia.org/wiki/List_of_trade_magazines

Press Releases

- PR Web – Permanently hosts your press releases and distributes to other sites. http://service.prweb.com/pricing/

- eReleases – Tips on writing and submitting press releases. http://www.ereleases.com/howtosubmit.html

- PR Log – Free online press release distribution service. http://www.prlog.org/submit-free-press-release.html

Newsletter Advertising

- Guide Star – Newsletter for nonprofits.
  http://www2.guidestar.org/rxg/news/newsletters/newsletter-advertising.aspx

- Entire Web – Newsletter on topics of search engine optimization, online business promotion, and advertising.
  http://www.entireweb.com/newsletter/advertise/

- B2B Magazine – Great advice on finding newsletters that take advertising and how to make your own attractive to outside advertisers.
  http://www.btobonline.com/apps/pbcs.dll/article?AID=/200 71112/FREE/71112001/1008/Email#seenit

Coupon Decks and Books

- ValPak – Advertise with other local retailers in this coupon deck mailer. http://www.valpak.com/advertise/

- MacRae's Blue Book – List of coupon distribution advertising services.
  http://www.macraesbluebook.com/search/product_compan y_list.cfm?prod_code=9000065

Receipt Advertising

- RTUI – Works with numerous grocery stores to print your advertisement on the back of cash register receipts.
  http://www.rtui.com

- Check the back of your receipts next time you make a purchase. The contact information for the company providing the advertising should be on there.

Direct Marketing

Direct Mail

- Melissa Data – Offers lists and comprehensive direct marketing services via email, mail, and fax. http://www.melissadata.com

- Info USA – Direct marketing via email and postcard; sales leads; lists. http://www.infousa.com

- United States Postal Service – Lots of information on DIY direct mail. http://www.usps.com/directmail/welcome.htm

- Vista Print – In addition to providing print services, Vista Print also offers database lists and direct mail pieces via postal service and email. http://www.vistaprint.com

Direct Marketing

- Association Execs – Association data and comprehensive listing of associations with contact information; database for sale. http://www.associationexecs.com/

- Voice Logic – Voice, fax, email broadcasting and call center services. http://www.voicelogic.com/

- Text Your Way to Profits – Presented by mobile guru Shaun Parsons, a comprehensive guide to text message marketing. https://www.aqua360.com/lp/text-your-way-to-profits/index.php

- Moto Message – SMS and text message marketing. http://www.motomessage.com/

- Telemarketing –Inbound and outbound call center services. http://www.telemarketing.com/

People Connections

- Trade Show News Network – Newsletter, tips, news, listing of annual events. http://www.tsnn.com/

- Biz Trade Shows – Comprehensive listing of global trade shows by industry. http://www.biztradeshows.com/trade-shows-by-industry.html

- Yahoo! Directory of Associations - http://dir.yahoo.com/business_and_economy/organizations/trade_associations/

- Web Source – Information, tips, and software to set up affiliate marketing for your company. http://www.web-source.net/affiliate_program.htm

- JAM – Affiliate marketing management system software. http://jam.jrox.com/

- Table Top Promotions – Partners with restaurants, hotels, and malls to put your advertisement on table tops. http://ttoppromos.com/

- Table Ads – Produces ads on restaurant tables only. http://www.tableads.com

- Microsoft – Create your own board game with a printer and Excel. http://www.microsoft.com/canada/home/memories-and-crafts/articles/all-a-board-create-a-personalized-board-game.aspx

- X Game Station – Complete kits for making your own video games. http://www.xgamestation.com/

- Guru – Find a freelance game developer/designer. http://www.guru.com/emp/search.aspx#&&page=1&lct=WorldRegion&search=Profiles&b=0--1&keyword=designer+game

- Ad Lab – Good resource for making your own advertising board games. http://adverlab.blogspot.com/2009/07/create-and-sell-your-own-board-games.html

Movie Theatre Advertising

- Screenvision – Marketing and media solutions for local and national movie theatre ads. http://www.screenvision.com/?gclid=CMe9scTfjKQCFQXs7QodkQ5uHw

- Yellow Pages – Find a list of your local movie theatres. http://www.yellowpages.com

David T. Fagan & Aaron Halderman

Chapter Twelve: An Advertising Crystal Ball – Media, Message, and Methodology of the Future

"We want to take that stupid little box we were forced into as advertisers, blow it up, and change the way we interact with the customer, and we want it to be around the experience." – Jim Farley, CMO of Ford

As we look forward to the future, what is modern advertising going to look like in the upcoming decades? It's really anybody's guess how advertising will evolve beyond the current social media craze, yet there are certain signs of things to come that give us a clue about how we will receive marketing messages in the future.

For one thing, the consumer is going to be more in control. We reviewed option advertising and the way that Hulu has made the first bold step in offering viewers a choice as to the content of the advertising they see. This trend is only going to grow. I predict that soon, every consumer will be able to choose options in every form of advertising – television, print, online, and satellite radio. The choices are going to be nearly limitless – requiring the need for increased creativity and resulting in popularity contests between competitors.

Markets are going to be more narrowly defined. Through data mining, advertisers can already glean a great deal of information only took eight years for half of all households to get a black and white television; the same number of years represents the reach of the internet.

An additional factor influencing the future of advertising is permission-based marketing. The focus is trending toward opt-ins, as discussed in the chapter on internet marketing. We've already seen how CAN-SPAM and the Do Not Call Registry have impacted advertising; future legislation could further cut into the number of opportunities available to commercial enterprises to bombard consumers with marketing messages. However, once you've got permission to communicate that message, you've got unlimited potential to submit, sway, and sell.

Sweeping and rapid technological advances are changing the forms of media to which consumers have access – and that is changing the effectiveness of traditional forms of advertising.

Take eBooks as an example. Traditional print publishers are now furiously modifying their business models to focus on digital books rather than soft- or hardbacks and with good reason. An eBook can be downloaded to a reading device, smartphone, notebook computer, PC, or PDA. And since all of these devices often include internet access, keywords within the book can become live links that take the reader directly to a website where that product or service is immediately available for purchase. Will the same thing happen with magazines and newspapers? There's no reason it couldn't.

I'm no techno geek, but I could certainly envision a day when print materials are merely flash drives that plug it into a computer or television set and enable readers to flip through the pages just as if it were a printed publication (which you can already do online with digital flipbooks). The same thing could certainly come true for movies; with the proliferation of wide screen TVs available at a reasonable price to the consumer, there is really no reason to go to a movie theatre other than a desire to watch the latest releases. But certainly production companies could make new releases available to the general public for a subscription fee and bypass theatres altogether.

And what about advertising agencies themselves? Currently, 80% of all advertising is provided by just four global companies. But those companies aren't needed any longer to negotiate favorable terms with media; the internet has leveled the playing field to the point that agencies are unnecessary for everything but the creative aspect of advertising. As I've shown in this book, even that is negligible. Any entrepreneur with a good sense of the company's target market can create an experiential campaign just as successful as the big ones included as The Moments that Changed Advertising in this book. Madison Avenue beware; in-house mad ads are erasing the industry's future potential.

The lesson here is that every business owner needs to keep up with rapidly developing changes and how it changes the way they reach prospective clients. There is no more "normal"; there is no more "traditional". And that's only going to continue as well as accelerate.

Be prepared now to face a future that is unlike any you've ever imagined when it comes to marketing your business. It's time to create a business advertising strategy that embraces the newest and most unique forms of establishing a relationship with your customers. Create mad ads and use the Law of Multiplication to put your company everywhere you cannot be – then watch your profits grow.